ENHANCING THE POSTDOCTORAL EXPERIENCE FOR SCIENTISTS AND ENGINEERS

A Guide for Postdoctoral Scholars,
Advisers, Institutions,
Funding Organizations, and Disciplinary
Societies

Committee on Science, Engineering, and Public Policy

NATIONAL ACADEMY OF SCIENCES
NATIONAL ACADEMY OF ENGINEERING
INSTITUTE OF MEDICINE

NATIONAL ACADEMY PRESS
Washington, DC

NATIONAL ACADEMY PRESS • 2101 Constitution Avenue, NW • Washington, DC 20418

NOTICE: This volume was produced as part of a project approved by the Governing Board of the National Research Council, whose members are drawn from the councils of the National Academy of Sciences, the National Academy of Engineering, and the Institute of Medicine. It is a result of work done by the Committee on Science, Engineering, and Public Policy (COSEPUP) as augmented, which has authorized its release to the public. This report has been reviewed by a group other than the authors according to procedures approved by COSEPUP and the Report Review Committee.

The **Committee on Science, Engineering, and Public Policy** (COSEPUP) is a joint committee of the NAS, the NAE, and the IOM. It includes members of the councils of all three bodies.

Financial Support: The development of this report was supported by the National Research Council, the Burroughs Wellcome Fund, the Howard Hughes Medical Institute, the Robert Wood Johnson Foundation, the National Institutes of Health, and the Sloan Foundation. The Howard Hughes Medical Institute does not assume responsibility for activities supported by the grant, for project results, or for their interpretation.

International Standard Book Number: 0-309-06996-3
Library of Congress Catalog Card Number 00-106115

Enhancing the Postdoctoral Experience for Scientists and Engineers is available from the National Academy Press, 2101 Constitution Ave., NW, P.O. Box 285, Washington, DC 20055. (1-800-624-6242 or 202/334-3313 in the Washington metropolitan area; Internet http://www.nap.edu). See www.nationalacademies.org/postdocs for further information.

Cover illustration by Leigh Coriale.

Printed in the United States of America

THE NATIONAL ACADEMIES

National Academy of Sciences
National Academy of Engineering
Institute of Medicine
National Research Council

The **National Academy of Sciences** is a private, nonprofit, self-perpetuating society of distinguished scholars engaged in scientific and engineering research, dedicated to the furtherance of science and technology and to their use for the general welfare. Upon the authority of the charter granted to it by the Congress in 1863, the Academy has a mandate that requires it to advise the federal government on scientific and technical matters. Dr. Bruce M. Alberts is president of the National Academy of Sciences.

The **National Academy of Engineering** was established in 1964, under the charter of the National Academy of Sciences, as a parallel organization of outstanding engineers. It is autonomous in its administration and in the selection of its members, sharing with the National Academy of Sciences the responsibility for advising the federal government. The National Academy of Engineering also sponsors engineering programs aimed at meeting national needs, encourages education and research, and recognizes the superior achievements of engineers. Dr. William A. Wulf is president of the National Academy of Engineering.

The **Institute of Medicine** was established in 1970 by the National Academy of Sciences to secure the services of eminent members of appropriate professions in the examination of policy matters pertaining to the health of the public. The Institute acts under the responsibility given to the National Academy of Sciences by its congressional charter to be an adviser to the federal government and, upon its own initiative, to identify issues of medical care, research, and education. Dr. Kenneth I. Shine is president of the Institute of Medicine.

The **National Research Council** was organized by the National Academy of Sciences in 1916 to associate the broad community of science and technology with the Academy's purposes of furthering knowledge and advising the federal government. Functioning in accordance with general policies determined by the Academy, the Council has become the principal operating agency of both the National Academy of Sciences and the National Academy of Engineering in providing services to the government, the public, and the scientific and engineering communities. The Council is administered jointly by both Academies and the Institute of Medicine. Dr. Bruce M. Alberts and Dr. William A. Wulf are chairman and vice chairman, respectively, of the National Research Council.

COMMITTEE ON SCIENCE, ENGINEERING, AND PUBLIC POLICY

---

* Ex officio member.

PROJECT GUIDANCE GROUP

MILDRED S. DRESSELHAUS, (*Chair*), Institute Professor of Electrical
Engineering and Physics, Massachusetts Institute of Technology, Cambridge
PETER DIAMOND, Institute Professor and Professor of Economics,
Massachusetts Institute of Technology, Cambridge
BRIGID HOGAN, Investigator, Howard Hughes Medical Institute and
Hortense B. Ingram Professor Department of Cell Biology, Vanderbilt
University School of Medicine, Nashville
SAMUEL H. PRESTON, Dean, School of Arts and Sciences, University of
Pennsylvania, Philadelphia
MAXINE SINGER, President, Carnegie Institution of Washington,
Washington, DC
IRVING L. WEISSMAN, Karele and Avice Beekhuis Professor of Cancer
Biology and Professor of Pathology, Stanford University School of Medicine,
Stanford, California

Principal Project Staff

DEBORAH D. STINE, Project Director
JAMES VOYTUK, Senior Program Officer, Office of Scientific
and Engineering Personnel
ELIZABETH HART, Research Associate
VIVIAN NOLAN, Research Associate
ELIZABETH SCHARL, National Academies Intern
ALAN ANDERSON, Consultant Science Writer
CHRIS FINDLAY, Editor
REBECCA BURKA, Administrative Associate
KEVIN ROWAN, Project Assistant

Preface

The Committee on Science, Engineering, and Public Policy (COSEPUP) has, for some time, been concerned with the many issues that surround the education and training of scientists and engineers in the United States. Its 1993 report, *Science, Technology, and the Federal Government: National Goals for a New Era,* emphasized the importance of human resources to the research enterprise. A second report, *Reshaping the Graduate Education of Scientists and Engineers* (1995), urged institutions to offer graduate students expanded educational experiences so that they would be better equipped to choose from among the broad range of careers now open to scientists and engineers. This report led to the development of one guide for students, *Careers in Science and Engineering: A Student Planning Guide to Grad School and Beyond* (1996), and another for their mentors, *Adviser, Teacher, Role Model, Friend: On Being a Mentor to Students in Science and Engineering* (1997). In the course of its work on these reports and guides, COSEPUP became increasingly aware of the need to also address the experiences of those who undertake additional research training after completing their doctoral degrees—the postdoctoral scholars, or postdocs. The present report is the result of the committee's intensive study of the postdoctoral experience. It is concerned largely with the personal and institutional settings of that experience. The core of a postdoc's world, the research effort that is at the center of the hugely successful US scientific and engineering research enterprise, is of course of primary importance, but it is not the subject of this guide.

During the past year, COSEPUP gathered information in meetings with a total of 39 groups of postdocs and advisers at 11 universities, seven national laboratories, and five private research institutes or industrial firms. In addition, the committee invited more than 100 postdocs, advisers, administrators, and others to a day-long workshop in Washington, DC (see Appendix D); conducted an electronic survey of research institutions (see Appendix C); met with the National Science Foundation (NSF) and the National Institutes of Health (NIH) staff; and consulted regularly with a 12-member External Advisory Group selected from institutions across the country. The informed and generous contributions of these groups are in large part responsible for COSEPUP's ability to document the characteristics of the postdoctoral experience. Besides reporting the committee's findings, this report suggests actions that can be taken to enhance the postdoctoral experience.

Although there is substantial variation in the experiences of postdocs from one field of science to another, certain elements are more-or-less common across the entire population. In the last 15 years, the number of postdocs has greatly increased and the nature of their experiences has changed in substantial ways. In some fields (e.g., life sciences), one or more postdoctoral experiences have become virtually mandatory for obtaining a regular position in academia or industry and the median time spent in postdoc positions has increased to 3.5 years. One reason for this is that graduate school programs cannot alone provide the broad range of knowledge and skills required for modern research. Another reason is that an extended postdoc period provides employment when regular positions are scarce compared to the number of students completing graduate degrees. A third reason is that postdocs want to accomplish work of substantial scope and significance in order to improve their chances of obtaining a desirable position.

Postdocs have become essential in many research settings. It is largely they who carry out the sometimes exhilarating, sometimes tedious day-to-day work. Their efforts account for a great deal of the extraordinary productivity of the United States' academic science and engineering enterprise. And yet the institutional status of postdocs, especially in academia, is often poorly defined. Consequently, although most postdocs value highly their experiences and the opportunity to engage in rewarding research without competing responsibilities, many of them are dissatisfied with their situations.

COSEPUP's analysis of the data gathered in this report indicates that the employment conditions for postdocs, especially in universities, need to be significantly improved if the United States is to develop the human capital needed to assure a healthy research enterprise and global leadership in science and technology. In many university settings, postdocs have uncertain status; they are neither faculty, staff, nor students. Consequently, there is often no clear administrative responsibility for assuring their fair compensation, benefits, or job security. Postdocs often receive no clear statement of the terms of their appointment and have no place to go to determine appropriate expectations or redress grievances. Often the sole person to whom they can turn for assistance is the Principal Investigator (PI) who hired them and upon whom they depend not only for support in their current position but also for help in advancing their careers. Given this dependence, a reluctance to be perceived as a complainer is understandable. In contrast to the postdocs, university graduate students, faculty, and staff function under clearly stated assumptions, including: definition of expectations, rights, and responsibilities, defined pay scales, periodic evaluations, defined benefits, benchmarks for pay increases, and established procedures for consideration of grievances.

Although the stipends of most postdocs derive from grants to their faculty advisers, major granting agencies, such as the NSF or NIH, provide few guidelines on the obligations of advisers or their institutions toward postdocs. Indeed, these agencies were not able to provide COSEPUP with dependable data about the number of postdocs (in their nomenclature, Research Associates) supported by grants, or about their salaries, benefits, or length of service.

There are several unfortunate outcomes of the rapid growth of the US postdoctoral population under these irregular conditions. The range of annual compensation for first-year postdocs spans tens of thousands of dollars per year, depending on field and type of institution. At the lower end of the range—which is typical of the life sciences in academia—the pay is embarrassingly low, especially for postdocs with families, when compared to that received by professionals in other fields at analogous career stages. There is no standard health benefit package for postdocs; some receive no health benefits for themselves, and many have no health coverage for their families.

COSEPUP recognizes that part of the compensation for postdocs is the further education and experience they receive and their freedom from responsibilities other than research. The committee learned that many postdocs do indeed have stimulating and productive research experiences under the supervision of attentive, sympathetic, and thoughtful mentors. However, we also learned about postdocs who are neglected, even exploited inappropriately, while making creative and fundamental contributions to the research projects on which they worked. The need to improve the postdoctoral experience has led some institutions to formulate policies to govern their employment. In other instances, postdocs themselves have formed organizations to promote their common interests. Other indications of serious dissatisfaction are the occasional discussions of unionization and even litigation; though rare, these more confrontational calls for action are at least a sign that reform is needed.

Reform efforts will have to be collaborative. While the postdocs themselves must play a role, the major responsibility for change lies with those who have the most power: the advisers, the research institutions, and the funding organizations. Disciplinary societies can play an important role in catalyzing and supporting the reform efforts, especially because the needed changes vary by field. All these participants will need to confront difficult questions in addition to the challenges already mentioned. For example, if mentors have insufficient grant funds to improve salaries and benefits, should they consider accepting fewer postdocs to allow for larger stipends? Also, what is the optimal length of time to be spent as a postdoc? Many are tempted to remain in their positions for five or more years because their experience and skill promise exciting breakthroughs and high productivity. Advisers may encourage long stays for the same reason, as well as because senior postdocs are particularly valuable in facilitating the education and training of graduate students and new postdocs. Junior researchers need to weigh the advantages and disadvantages of remaining overly long as postdocs against those associated with alternative opportunities. COSEPUP suggests that postdocs who remain in their positions for more than five years be reclassified as regularly employed researchers. Aside from personal considerations, there may be costs to the research enterprise itself if relatively junior researchers postpone their independence and are unable to apply their energies in the pursuits of their own original ideas.

Excellent postdoctoral experiences for new scientists and engineers are critical to the health and productivity of current and future research. High school, undergraduate, and graduate students need positive messages about scientific and engineering education and research careers if they are to continue pursuing their scientific and engineering interests. There are many marvelous aspects to the present system. It is essential that this highly productive relationship between research and education be continued under optimal conditions.

Maxine Singer

Chair
Committee on Science,
Engineering, and Public Policy

Acknowledgements

A guidance group consisting of Mildred S. Dresselhaus (Chair), Peter Diamond, Brigid Hogan, Samuel H. Preston, Maxine Singer, and Irving L. Weissman supervised the preparation of the guide.

Valuable feedback was provided by an external advisory group composed of:

- Patricia Bresnahan, Molecular Dynamics and recent postdoctoral scholar at the University of California, San Francisco;
- Jerry Bryant, Director, United Negro College Fund–Merck Initiative;
- Joseph Cerny, Vice Chancellor for Research and Sam Castaneda, Post-doctoral Programs Director, University of California, Berkeley;
- Michael Cowan, Office of Student Services, Stanford University;
- Susan Duby, Director, Division of Graduate Studies, National Science Foundation;
- Jean Labus, Senior Personnel Representative, Postdoctoral Programs, Eli Lilly and Co.;
- Trevor Penning, Associate Dean for Postdoctorate Training, University of Pennsylvania School of Medicine;
- Patricia Roth, Abbott Laboratories and recent postdoctoral scholar;
- Walter Schaffer, Research Training Officer, National Research Service Awards Program, National Institutes of Health;
- Marion Thurnauer, Director, Chemistry Division, Argonne National Laboratory;
- Letitia Yao, Postdoctoral Scholar, University of Minnesota; and
- Michael Zigmond, Professor, Department of Neurology, University of Pittsburgh.

This group of experts consulted regularly via conference call to provide comments on drafts of the guide and the survey.

The committee extends special thanks to the informed and enthusiastic participants at its day-long workshop in Washington, DC; to participants in its workshop with disciplinary societies who provided a better understanding of how the postdoctoral experience varies by discipline; and to the several hundred postdocs, faculty, advisers, administrators, and federal agency staff who generously offered their opinions, critiques, and personal experiences at 39 focus groups held around the country. These individuals and organizations are identified in appendixes C, D, and E.

We would like to express a special thanks to administrators at the institutions listed below who took time out of their busy schedules to carefully respond to our electronic survey:

Academic Institutions
Arizona State University
Columbia University
Cornell University
Harvard University
Indiana University
Iowa State University
Massachusetts Institute of Technology
Stanford University
Tennessee State University
The University of Michigan
The University of Texas at Austin
University of California, Berkeley
University of California, Los Angeles
University of California, San Diego
University of California, San Francisco
University of Cincinnati
University of Colorado, Boulder
University of Minnesota
University of North Carolina, Chapel Hill
University of Washington
University of Wisconsin, Madison
Virginia Polytechnic Institute and State University
Washington University
Yale University

Medical Schools
Johns Hopkins School of Medicine
New York University School of Medicine

University of Medicine and Dentistry of New Jersey
University of Pennsylvania School of Medicine
University of Toronto, Faculty of Medicine
Yeshiva University, Albert Einstein College of Medicine

National Laboratories
Los Alamos National Laboratory
Environmental Protection Agency
National Oceanic and Atmospheric Administration
US Army Research Laboratory

Industry
Eli Lilly and Company
Microsoft Corporation
Parke-Davis

Research Institutes
Chemical Industry Institute of Toxicology
Fred Hutchinson Cancer Research Center
Rowland Institute for Science

This guide has been reviewed in draft form by individuals chosen for their diverse perspectives and technical expertise, in accordance with procedures approved by the National Research Council's Report Review Committee. The purpose of this independent review is to provide candid and critical comments that will assist the institution in making the published report as sound as possible and to ensure that the report meets institutional standards for objectivity, evidence, and responsiveness to the study charge. The review comments and draft manuscript remain confidential to protect the integrity of the deliberative process. We wish to thank the following individuals for their participation in the review of this report:

R. Stephen Berry, University of Chicago
Patsy Brannon, Cornell University
Sarah Caddick, Cancer Research Fund
Roger Chalkley, Vanderbilt University Medical Center
Ellis Cowling, North Carolina State University
Stephen Cross, Carnegie Mellon University
Nancy Dess, American Psychological Association
Peter Fiske, Lawrence Livermore National Laboratory
Nick Gaiano, New York University School of Medicine
David Goodstein, California Institute of Technology

Sherrie Hans, Pew Charitable Trusts
Marc Kirschner, Harvard Medical School
Jeffrey Krause, University of Florida
Henry Kronenberg, Massachusetts General Hospital
Randall Kuhn, RAND Corporation
Jules LaPidus, Council of Graduate Schools
Lisa McCawley, Vanderbilt University
Richard McGee, Mayo Graduate School
Joel Oppenheim, New York University School of Medicine
Trevor Penning, University of Pennsylvania
Elizabeth Powell, University of Pittsburgh
Monique Rijnkels, Baylor College of Medicine
William Schowalter, University of Illinois
Thomas Smith, Howard University
Teresa Sullivan, University of Texas at Austin
Shirley Tilghman, Princeton University
Michael Zigmond, University of Pittsburgh

Finally, we would like to thank the staff for this project including Deborah Stine, Associate Director of COSEPUP and Project Director; Jim Voytuk, Senior Program Officer, NRC Office of Scientific and Engineering Personnel, who analyzed the quantitative data on postdocs; Elizabeth Hart, Research Associate, who worked with COSEPUP in developing the survey of institutions and arranged the focus groups; Vivian Nolan, Research Associate, who analyzed the results of the survey; Elizabeth Scharl, National Academies Intern, who helped with the initial research; Alan Anderson, Consultant Writer, who worked with COSEPUP to develop the text of the guide; Stephanie Dawson, Intern, who helped develop COSEPUP's postdoc webguide; Rebecca Burka, Administrative Associate, who provided support for the workshop and other activities; Kevin Rowan, Administrative Assistant; and Richard Bissell, Executive Director of COSEPUP.

A Note on Using This Guide

This guide addresses five primary populations, all of whom participate in the postdoctoral experience: the postdocs themselves, their advisers, their host institutions, the agencies and organizations that support them, and professional disciplinary societies. It is also intended for senior-level graduate students who may be contemplating postdoctoral work.

At the risk of some repetition, the guide addresses the primary groups in separate sections because of differences in perspective, primary objectives, and responsibilities. For those readers who wish to skim material addressed to other groups, each section contains a summary of its main points.

The text is arranged in the following manner:

- Chapter 1 summarizes the trends that have brought growth and new stresses to the postdoctoral population and provides a description of **postdoctoral scholars in the United States.**
- Chapter 2 describes prominent **features of the postdoctoral experience**.
- Chapter 3 outlines the **rights, opportunities, and responsibilities of postdocs.**
- Chapter 4 addresses the relationship between the **postdoc and the adviser.**
- Chapter 5 describes the relationship between **postdocs and the institutions** where they work.
- Chapter 6 provides an overview of how **funding organizations** provide financial support to postdocs.
- Chapter 7 summarizes the role of professional **disciplinary societies** in supporting the postdoctoral experience.

- Chapter 8 provides a series of **principles, action points, and recommendations** for enhancing the postdoctoral experience for the benefit of all participants.

Throughout the guide appear boxes highlighting "Best Practices" we have seen among various institutions and organizations. This series of "Best Practices" boxes explores the postdoc-adviser research relationship; their fictional scenarios are based on discussions from our focus groups. In addition, the actual experiences of two recent postdocs are profiled.

Additional boxes summarize highlights of the institutional survey we conducted, as illustrated below (see Box). Note that some questions requested multiple responses. More information on the survey is provided in Appendix C. We encourage institutions to use the guide as a basis for dialog among all the populations it addresses. Discussion of the postdoctoral experience can occur in many settings, including:

- Orientation sessions
- Career counseling offices
- Departmental or school "practice of science" symposia
- Job fairs and conventions
- Student discussion or support groups
- Professional society meetings
- Meetings between advisers and graduate students or postdocs
- Information interviews
- Management meetings (e.g., faculty senate, department, school)

How Many Postdocs Are Currently Serving Appointments at This Organization?

Nearly 18 percent of respondents reported postdoctoral populations of more than 1000. Institutions reported smaller populations as follows:

Fewer than 50	15%
50-100	18%
101-250	21%
251-500	8%
501-750	5%
751-1000	15%

COSEPUP Survey Results

For those developing plans to enhance the postdoctoral experience, COSEPUP has developed a web site—www.nationalacademies.org/postdocs—which includes the full text of this guide, a one-page summary of the guide, and links to the web sites of institutions we suggest provide exemplary "Best Practices." These best-practice models can be helpful to postdocs, postdoc advisers, institutions, funding organizations, and disciplinary societies as they explore ways to enhance the postdoctoral experience.

Contents

xix

Figures, Tables, and Boxes

FIGURES

xxiii

TABLES

BOXES

Best Practices

Practice Descriptions

Profiles

Best Practice Scenarios

COSEPUP Survey Results

Executive Summary

The concept of a postdoctoral scholar in science and engineering arose about a century ago when a handful of PhD researchers were awarded small stipends for the purpose of augmenting their skills and experience. The postdoctoral population in the United States, after decades of gradual growth, leapt ahead quickly in the 1980s and now outnumbers the graduate student population at some US institutions. The total number of postdoctoral scholars, or postdocs, has grown to an estimated 52,000.

The primary purpose of the postdoctoral experience is to broaden and deepen the research and other skills that are required for a significant contribution to society and satisfying, professional employment. Ideally, this is accomplished through the guidance of an adviser in whose laboratory or department the postdoc works; the administrative and infrastructural support of the host institution; the financial support of a funding organization; and the professional development support of a disciplinary society.

The postdoctoral experience does not always succeed in its educational purpose. In some cases, the postdoc is poorly matched with the research setting; in others, there is little opportunity for growth toward independence, guidance is poor, or a mentoring relationship fails to develop. Sometimes mentors, institutions, and funding organizations have been slow to assign postdocs the status, recognition, and compensation that are commensurate with their skills and contributions to research.

For their part, many postdocs express frustration at their low professional status and inability to fulfill their own expectations to mature as professional researchers, collaborate productively with colleagues (and advisers), and advance

1

in their careers toward rewarding professional positions. While some of this frustration results from a job market that, in some fields, has fewer positions than it does good candidates, it also reflects inadequate administrative attention to mechanisms of the experience that can and should be rectified. In considering needed improvements, it is essential to recognize that the situations of postdocs vary markedly from discipline to discipline and between academic and non-academic settings. Postdocs vary in proficiency; some are quite experienced with little need for guidance, while others are apprentices who require substantial coaching. They also vary in their rate of growth; some learn quickly while others require more time to develop sufficient knowledge and skills to move to the next stage of their career. Moreover, slightly more than half of US postdocs are non-US citizens, many of whom face additional challenges of acculturation and language.

GUIDING PRINCIPLES

After extensive interviews, workshops, and deliberations, COSEPUP drew up a series of recommendations for all participants in the postdoctoral experience—postdocs, their advisers, host institutions, funding organizations, and disciplinary societies. These recommendations are based on the following guiding principles:

1. The postdoctoral experience is first and foremost a period of apprenticeship for the purpose of gaining scientific, technical, and professional skills that advance the professional career.

2. Postdocs should receive appropriate recognition (including lead author credit) and compensation (including health insurance and other fringe benefits) for the contributions they make to the research enterprise.

3. To ensure that postdoctoral appointments are beneficial to all concerned, all parties to the appointments—the postdoc, the postdoc adviser, the host institution, and funding organizations—should have a clear and mutually-agreed-upon understanding with regard to the nature and purpose of the appointment.

TEN ACTION POINTS

In order to enhance the postdoctoral experience, advisers, institutions, funding organizations, and disciplinary societies should:

1. Award institutional recognition, status, and compensation commensurate with the contributions of postdocs to the research enterprise.

2. Develop distinct policies and standards for postdocs, modeled on those available for graduate students and faculty.

3. Develop mechanisms for frequent and regular communication between postdocs and their advisers, institutions, funding organizations, and disciplinary societies.

4. Monitor and provide formal evaluations (at least annually) of the performance of postdocs.

5. Ensure that all postdocs have access to health insurance, regardless of funding source, and to institutional services.

6. Set limits for total time of a postdoc appointment (of approximately five years, summing time at all institutions), with clearly described exceptions as appropriate.

7. Invite the participation of postdocs when creating standards, definitions, and conditions for appointments.

8. Provide substantive career guidance to improve postdocs' ability to prepare for regular employment.

9. Improve the quality of data both for postdoctoral working conditions and for the population of postdocs in relation to employment prospects in research.

10. Take steps to improve the transition of postdocs to regular career positions.

1

Postdoctoral Scholars in US Institutions

Since the 1960s, the performance of research in the United States has relied more and more on graduate scientists and engineers who have recently earned a PhD or equivalent doctorate and are pursuing further education and training in their field or learning a new specialty. These postdoctoral scholars, or postdocs, work on a full-time but temporary basis for one or more years to gain additional research experience in preparation for a professional research career. Figure 1-1[1] shows that the vast majority of all postdocs who received doctorates at US institutions work in universities (approximately 80 percent), with smaller percentages working in government (13 percent) and industry (7 percent). The number of postdoctoral scholars has increased in all sectors since 1981. Within academia (see Table 1-1) 272 institutions have postdocs, with the largest number concentrated at the research-intensive institutions.

Population growth. The roots of the postdoctoral phenomenon reach back just over a century to the 1870s, when high-level apprenticeships became part of the new European-modeled research institution. Johns Hopkins University adopted the apprenticeship model shortly after its founding in 1876, and in the 1920s the Rockefeller Foundation established formal postdoctoral fellowships in physical science, recognizing that physics had become too complex to learn within the time limits of traditional programs.

The hiring of postdocs grew only modestly during the first half of the twentieth century. The first period of rapid growth began in the late 1950s, when the

---

[1]The data for the figures and a detailed description of the data sources for the tables and figures in the guide can be found in Appendix B.

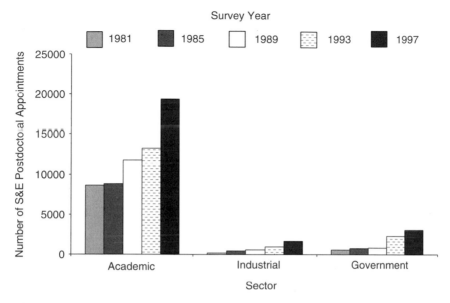

FIGURE 1-1: Total Number of Postdoctoral Appointments in the Life Sciences, Engineering, Physics, Chemistry, and the Social/Behavioral Sciences, by Sector, 1981-1997. Source: 1981, 1985, 1989, 1993, and 1997 Survey of Doctorate Recipients.

Cold War stimulated federal spending and a sudden demand for scientists and engineers. PhDs awarded in science and engineering approximately tripled from 1960-1970.[2] Increasingly, those completing graduate school (20-30 percent in most sciences, 50 percent in biomedicine) took postdoc positions to broaden or deepen their experience before moving to faculty or other research career opportunities. The nation's laboratories began to count on this new corps of skilled, low-cost apprentices to increase the productivity and quality of research.

By the end of that decade growth had slowed. In the early 1970s the baby boom cohort passed through the system, recession came, and the government reduced support of graduate fellowships quite abruptly.[3] The smaller pool of graduate students left laboratories short-handed and, partly as a response, the number of non-US graduate students increased.

---

[2]Fechter, A. E., and Gaddy, C. D. "Trends in Doctoral Education and Employment." *Higher Education: Handbook of Theory and Research,* Vol. XIII. New York: Agathon Press, 1998.

[3]Breneman, D. W. *Graduate School Adjustments to the 'New Depression' in Higher Education.* National Board on Graduate Education Technical Report No. 3. Washington, DC: National Academy of Sciences, 1975.

TABLE 1-1: Top 25 Academic Institutions with the Largest Total Number of Postdoctoral Appointments in 1998

Institution	Astronomy	Chemistry	Physics	Biological Sciences
All Academic Institutions	**357**	**3,716**	**1,859**	**15,480**
Top 25				
Harvard University	11	115	44	1,003
University of Calif at San Francisco				319
Stanford University		72	7	423
Johns Hopkins University	53	23		292
University of Calif at San Diego		86	54	269
University of Washington	6	28	24	439
University of Calif at Berkeley	35	169	24	475
University of Pennsylvania		52	45	302
University of California, Los Angeles		85	38	213
Duke University		29		293
University of Michigan	8	37	30	183
University of Colorado	36	67		163
Washington University		35	13	281
Univ of North Carolina at Chapel Hill		60	16	218
Cornell University		63	48	156
University of Minnesota	6	47	21	249
University of Southern California		45	5	125
University of Arizona	51	40	36	188
California Institute of Technology	21	96	54	170
University of Wisconsin-Madison	2	42	17	171
Massachusetts Institute of Technology		78	20	127
Indiana University		36	22	156
Baylor College of Medicine				257
Univ of Texas SW Medical Ctr at Dallas				277
Univ of Texas M.D. Anderson Cancer Ctr			2	233

Source: 1998 Survey of Graduate Students and Postdoctorates in Science and Engineering

A changing pattern. By the late 1970s, the pattern of postdoctoral behavior began to change. Numbers of postdocs increased as PhD labor markets weakened. The time spent as postdocs began to lengthen, suggesting difficulty in finding jobs. A substantial number of those receiving PhDs reported that they became postdocs because they had few other options.[4]

Employment conditions improved somewhat in the mid- and late 1980s, but

---

[4]Zumeta, W. *Extending the Educational Ladder: The Changing Quality and Value of Postdoctoral Study.* Lexington, MA: D. C. Heath/Lexington Books, 1985.

Earth, Atmospheric and Ocean Sciences	Engineering	Health Sciences	Mathematical & Computer Sciences	Psychology	Social Sciences	Total All Disciplines
897	**2,830**	**12,137**	**642**	**612**	**383**	**39,619**
15	46	2,110	8	25	24	3,407
		834		11	1	1,165
20	77	459	10	21		1,089
4	45	551	5	21	12	1,006
80	66	363	21	17	26	982
15	44	368	7	9	1	953
14	87	77	16	16	32	945
3	39	401	42	5	15	904
14	67	375	2	13	6	813
6	28	342	6	11	10	730
22	45	311	1	4	6	647
41	48	246	17	13		631
8	7	272	2	2	3	623
17	1	238	1	1	7	559
6	81	156	5	8	2	554
20	70	101	3	5	3	539
15	31	225	24	3	6	479
43	63	29	9	12		478
33	89		6		2	471
22	45	100	1	10	13	465
30	102	47	7	42	3	456
5	4	127	7	23	28	408
		149				406
		123				400
		162		2		399

the recession of the early 1990s brought longer-lasting sluggishness and caution in university hiring.[5] With limited permanent job prospects, the population of postdocs reached unprecedented size[6] and postdoctoral terms lengthened.[7]

[5]Zumeta, W. "State Higher Education Finance and Policy Developments: 1997." *The NEA 1998 Almanac of Higher Education.* Washington, DC: National Education Association, 1998.

[6]Association of American Universities. Committee on Postdoctoral Education, *Report and Recommendations.* Washington, DC, 1998.

[7]Regets, M. "Has the Use of Postdocs Changed?" National Science Foundation, Division of Science Resources Studies *Issue Brief.* NSF 99-310, 1999.

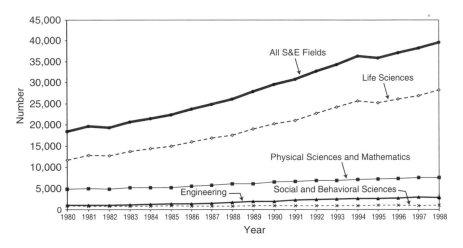

FIGURE 1-2: Postdoctoral Appointees in Academic Institutions by Broad Fields, 1980-1998. Source: Survey of Graduate Students and Postdoctorates in Science and Engineering, 1980-1998.

Meanwhile the number of non-US graduate students and new PhDs in science and engineering leveled off in the early 1990s having grown for many years.

Overall, the most significant growth in the postdoctoral population has taken place in the last 15 years (Figure 1-1). According to data gathered by the National Science Foundation (NSF), the number of postdocs in university departments of science and engineering more than doubled between 1981 and 1998, rising from approximately 18,000 to 39,000 (see Figure 1-2). A figure for the exact population of science and engineering postdocs across all sectors (including government and the private sector) is not available, but it is estimated to be approximately 52,000.[8] Slightly more than half of these postdocs are non-US citizens.

It is difficult to predict whether this upward trend will continue. Figure 1-3 provides a history of the number of doctorates who are planning postdoctoral study compared to the total number of doctorates for the three fields that account for most of the postdocs in science and engineering: biological science, chemis-

---

[8]Figure 1-2 only provides information for postdoctoral scholars who received their degrees from US universities. No source of data includes all sectors that employ postdoctoral scholars regardless of where they received their degree. This is important, given the large number of postdoctoral scholars who come to the United States from other countries. However, a rough estimate can be made by comparing data from several NSF sources (see Appendix E for discussion of sources). In 1997, the last year for which sector data exists, the number of postdoctoral appointments in academic institutions was 73 percent of the total appointments across all sectors. From the 39,619 academic appointments one can infer a total population of about 52,000.

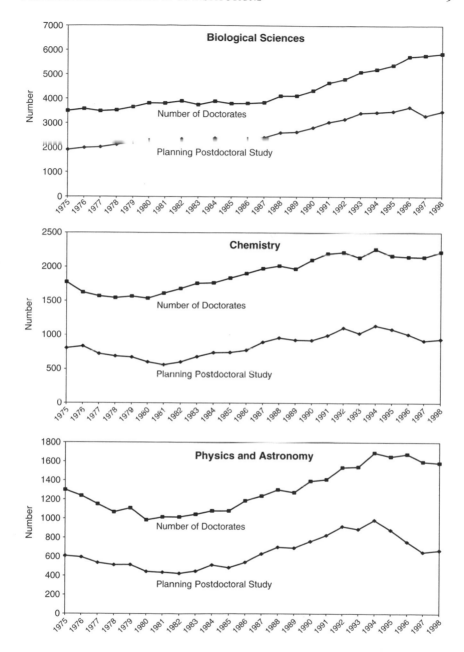

FIGURE 1-3: Number of Doctorates and the Number Planning Postdoctoral Study, 1975-1998, by Field. Source: 1975-1998 Survey of Earned Doctorates.

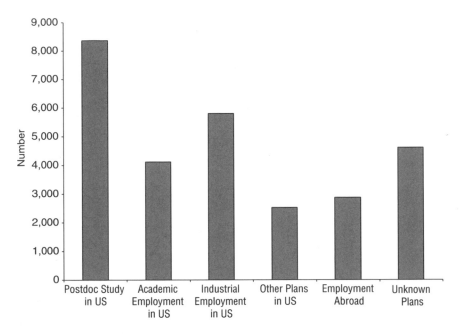

FIGURE 1-4: Postgraduation Plans of Science and Engineering Doctorates at the Time They Received Their Degree, 1998. Source: 1998 Survey of Earned Doctorates.

try, and physics/astronomy. Interestingly, the proportion of doctorates planning postdoctoral study was roughly constant from 1975-1994. However, beginning around 1994 the trends were no longer parallel, as a declining number of recent US doctorates have been planning postdoctoral study in the three fields examined.

The importance of postdocs to research. As a whole, the postdoctoral population has become indispensable to the science and engineering enterprise, performing a substantial portion of the nation's research in every setting. For example, a survey of research articles in two recent issues of *Science* found that 43 percent of the first authors were postdocs.[9] In many labs, postdocs also educate, train, and supervise junior members, help write grant proposals and papers, and present the laboratory's research results at professional society meetings. More than 15 universities have postdoctoral populations that exceed 500 (see Table 1-1).

Postdoctoral experiences are increasingly seen as central to careers in research. As illustrated in Figure 1-4, about 40 percent of the 1998 doctorates that plan to remain in the US will enter postdoctoral study rather than regular employment.

---

[9]Vogel, G. *Science,* 1999, Vol. 285, p. 1531.

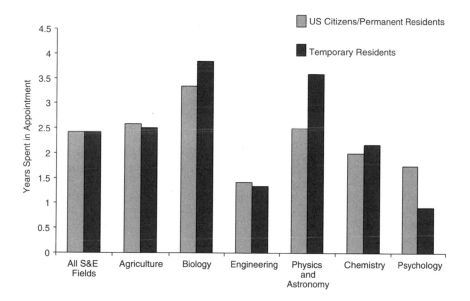

FIGURE 1-5: Median Number of Years Spent in Postdoctorate Appointment for Doctorates in the 1989-1991 Year Cohort, by Degree Field and Citizenship at Time of Degree. Source: 1997 Survey of Doctorate Recipients.

A postdoctoral appointment is a virtual prerequisite for those wishing to carry out long-term, independent research in the life sciences, physics, chemistry, and a growing number of other fields.[10] In addition, postdocs with experience in non-research settings (e.g., AAAS Congressional fellowships, National Academies internships) can substantially enhance their potential for employment in government and non-governmental organizations.

Postdoctoral terms. The length of a postdoc term varies by field (see Figure 1-5). Biologists tend to stay on the longest (five years is common), engineers the shortest (a year is common). Postdoc terms for physical scientists are usually two or, at most, three years, but some physical scientists work as postdocs for six years, while a small percentage of researchers extend their postdoctoral terms indefinitely. There is no difference in the time spent in a postdoctoral position

---

[10]Nearly a decade ago, Steven Sample, president of the University of Southern California and chair of the Postdoctoral Education Committee of the Association of American Universities, stated that "...in an increasing number of fields, the postdoctorate is becoming the terminal credential, with the result that the PhD in those fields, while still very important, is becoming *de facto* an interim milestone." See: AAU, Committee on Postdoctoral Education, *Report and Recommendations,* Washington, DC: March 31, 1998.

How Is the Duration of a Postdoctoral Appointment Determined?

Responses to this question were divided fairly evenly. The largest number (58 percent) reported that the duration of an appointment may be determined primarily by the adviser at any time during the appointment. Almost as many (55 percent) reported that duration is determined primarily by the source of funding and/or funding availability. Some 45 percent reported that duration is determined before a postdoc's arrival.

Many institutions reported firm limits on postdoctoral terms (typically 3, 4, or 5 years). Others allowed for extensions "in special cases," which sometimes required the approval of an administration officer. Other policies were 1) to appoint postdocs for a year at a time, with renewal depending on funding and performance, and 2) to allow the length of training to vary by field and source of funding, with no suggested limit.

COSEPUP Survey Results

when viewed from the perspective of citizenship for all science and engineering doctoral fields, but in the biological sciences, chemistry, and especially in physics temporary residents spend longer periods in postdoctoral positions. The 1998 Association of American Universities report[11] recommended limiting the total postdoctoral experience to six years; some universities now impose five-year limits, with exceptions for such circumstances as illness, childbirth, a need for exposure to multiple fields, or a need to finish a project that is in an advanced stage. The COSEPUP survey results suggest that institutions have a wide variety of policies on postdoctoral terms, and many institutions allow the adviser to determine the length of the term at any time during the appointment (see Box).

Multiple postdoctoral positions. In some fields, such as neuroscience, genetics, and epidemiology, more than one postdoctoral position may be useful to gain multidisciplinary expertise. In other fields, a tight job market forces some researchers to complete two or even three postdoctoral appointments while they hunt for jobs. In some cases, multiple postdoctoral appointments may bring many years of low compensation and a lack of security and stability that is demoralizing and stressful. This is of special concern for postdocs with families. In other cases, researchers may continue beyond their postdoctoral term to spend their careers in successive soft-money positions they find challenging and rewarding.

Unmet expectations. By design, the experience of postdocs should be professionally productive and career enhancing. For many of them, however, the

---

[11]AAU, Committee on Postdoctoral Education, *Report and Recommendations,* 1998.

TABLE 1-2: Comparison of Postdoc Annual Median Earnings with Other Populations, 1997-1998

Population	Annual Median Earnings
Minimum Wage (4)	$10,300
Poverty Level, family of 2 (3)	$11,060
Poverty Level, family of 4 (3)	$16,700
Administrative Support, all workers (4)	$24,120
All US workers (1)	$26,150
POSTDOCTORAL SCHOLARS, Academic sector, within 6 years of PhD (2)	$28,000
POSTDOCTORAL SCHOLARS, All sectors, within 6 years of PhD (2)	$30,000
Technical Support, all workers (1)	$32,420
Bachelor's degree recipient, 25-34 years old (1)	$35,030
POSTDOCTORAL SCHOLARS, Industry sector, within 6 years of PhD (2)	$36,000
POSTDOCTORAL SCHOLARS, Government sector, within 6 years of PhD (2)	$37,000
Public school classroom teacher, average, all workers (1)	$40,130
Master's degree recipient, 25-34 years old (1)	$40,800
Assistant Professor, Science & Engineering, within 6 years of PhD (2)	$42,800
Doctorate degree recipient, 25-34 years old (1)	$47,780
Professional degree recipient, 25-34 years old (1)	$58,080

Sources:
1. *Statistical Abstract of the United States,* 1999, Tables 266, 282, 702, and 703 and refer to the time period, 1997-1998.
2. 1997 Survey of Doctorate Recipients.
3. Federal Register, Vol. 64, No. 52, March 18, 1999, pp. 13428-13430.
4. www.dol.gov/dol/esa/public/minwage/main.htm

Notes:
• This analysis should be viewed as only a rough approximation. For comparison purposes, all analyses are on the basis of 40 hours/week, 50 weeks/year in the 1997-1998 timeframe.
• Benefits are not included above. The degree to which postdoctoral scholars receive benefits varies widely.

experience falls short of expectations. They often fail to achieve the recognition, standing, or compensation that is commensurate with their experience and skills (See Table 1-2 for salary comparisons). It is not uncommon for postdocs to hold uncertain standing in the institutions where they work, to receive inadequate mentoring or technical supervision and, in some fields, to accept stipends and benefits substantially below those of their professional peers in academia, government, or industry, as well as below those of non-PhD technicians. Some researchers continue to be categorized as "postdocs" for a decade or more after completing their doctorate.

Many postdocs voice frustration at not finding the kinds of positions they anticipated—notably, academic positions—when they began their many years of graduate and postdoctoral education. According to the Survey of Doctoral Recipients, the opportunities for doctorates and postdoctorates to move into faculty positions have decreased significantly since 1987 (see Figure 1-6 for the ratio of tenured faculty positions to number of doctorates). A substantial minority of postdocs in all fields reported difficulty in finding the jobs they wanted, and that the reason for taking a first postdoctoral appointment was that "other employment was not available" (see Figure 1-7). The NRC's *Trends* report on the life sciences noted a 42 percent increase in PhD production between 1987 and 1996 that "was not accompanied by a parallel increase in employment opportunities."[12] The report stated that many recent graduates who are unable to find full-time positions use the postdoctoral experience as a "holding pattern."[13]

Similarly, an on-line survey of Baylor University School of Medicine's postdocs in 1997 indicated that 34 percent had prolonged their terms because of difficulty in finding other employment; only 6 percent reported a "permanent career position that will start in the next 12 months."[14]

Variations by field and sector. It is difficult, however, to draw broad conclusions about postdoctoral experiences, which vary widely by field and by sector. In some fields, such as computer science and engineering, there is relatively little incentive to pursue a postdoc—or even a PhD—because rewarding jobs are available at the bachelor's and master's levels. In other fields, such as biology and physics, a postdoc is virtually mandatory, especially for academic employment. Some postdocs, especially in government or industrial laboratories, are paid better than some junior faculty. Stipends for academic postdocs, however, especially in the life sciences and chemistry, may be $15,000 to $20,000 lower than for government or industry postdocs (Figure 1-8). Even within a single discipline, experiences differ across advisers, programs, employment sectors, and geographic regions.

At its focus groups and workshop discussions, COSEPUP heard lively debates on the quality of the postdoc experience (see Appendixes). There was little disagreement about the potential value of research activities—almost all discussants agreed that the postdoctoral period can be one of the most professionally

---

[12]Office of Scientific and Engineering Personnel, National Research Council, *Trends in the Early Careers of Life Scientists*. Washington, DC: National Academy Press, 1998.

[13]The report states: "The frustration of young [life] scientists caught in the holding pattern is understandable. These people, most of whom are 35-40 years old, typically receive low salaries and have little job security or status within the university. Moreover, they are competing with a rapidly growing pool of highly talented young scientists—including many highly qualified foreign postdoctoral fellows—for a limited number of jobs...."

[14]See www.bcm.tmc.edu/pda/reference/proposal.html

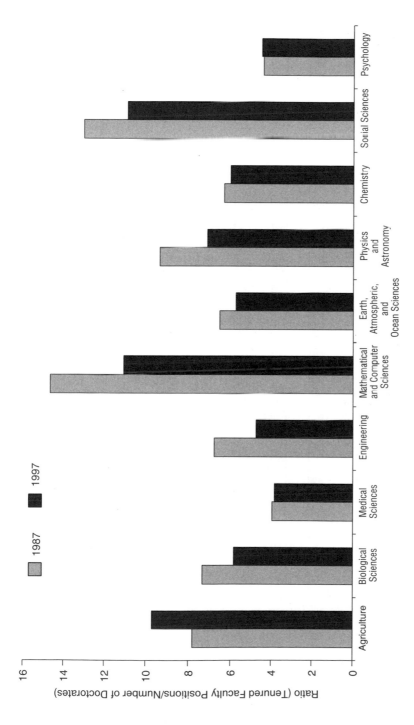

FIGURE 1-6: Ratio of the Number of Tenured Faculty to the Number of New Doctorates Awarded in 1987 and 1997 Source: 1987 and 1997 Survey of Doctorate Recipients.

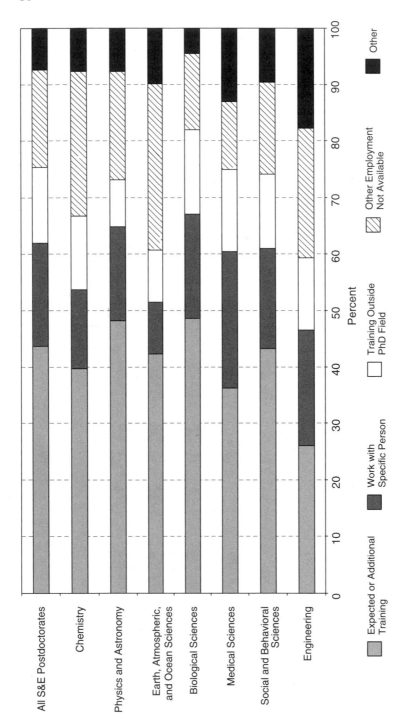

FIGURE 1-7: Reasons for Taking First Postdoctoral Appointment, by Field of Doctorate, 1997. Source: Survey of Doctorate Recipients, 1997.

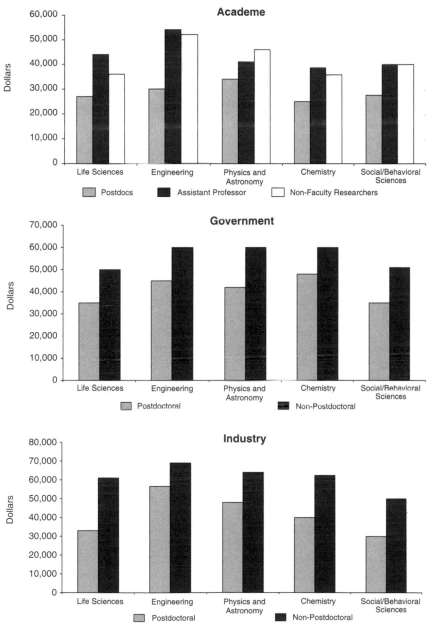

Note: Non-faculty researchers are full-time academic personnel who do not have faculty rank and indicate that their primary work activity is pure or applied research. Non-postdoctoral personnel in industry and government are individuals who hold full-time positions.

FIGURE 1-8: Median Salaries in 1997 for Doctorates in the Six-Year PhD Cohort, 1991-1996, by Field, Sector, and Type of Appointment. Source: 1997 Survey of Doctorate Recipients

rewarding of their lives. The debate focused instead on institutional standing, compensation, benefits, and other issues, which cause many postdocs to question the value of the experience. As some indicated, the lost-opportunity costs of forsaking other employment begin to outweigh the benefits of an otherwise fulfilling experience.

Some postdoc advisers and representatives of funding organizations indicated that the low compensation received by many postdocs is justified because it is offset by the benefits of supervised education and training.[15] Some postdocs, however, stated that they are regarded primarily as a "skilled pair of hands" that support the work of the principal investigator (PI), rather than as junior colleagues who only require further education and training to move toward their own research independence.

Increasing age. Issues of standing and compensation are exacerbated by the increasing age of the postdoctoral population. Today's junior scientists and engineers take longer to complete their doctorates (the average PhD recipient in the life sciences is 32 years old),[16] and many then take two or even three postdoctoral positions. In the Baylor survey, 67 percent of respondents were over age 30 and 21 percent were over age 35; 46 percent had children. The NSF reports a similar picture among the postdocs it funds (see further discussion in Chapter 2). Although many postdocs have families that include children, few institutions or funding organizations provide family health insurance, child care, or other family benefits received by others of similar professional stature. The same is true of their salary (Table 1-2).

A debate over responsibility. Another debate that emerged during focus groups concerned whether the host institution or the funding organization bears the primary responsibility for providing benefits and oversight for the postdoc.

Some PI's are reluctant to increase the salaries of their postdocs due to limited funds and the possible reduction in the number of postdocs they could fund. Even if they wish to do so, postdoc advisers indicated they face barriers from both the institution and the funding organization at the proposal acceptance stage *and* once funding is received. Some major funding organizations stated that institutions are directly responsible because they set salary compensation levels and receive funding (as a designated portion of each grant) from which to provide fringe benefits. Many institutions contend that funding organizations are primarily responsible, because they set the standard at which most postdocs are compensated. In particular, many universities use the scale NIH has developed for its National Research Service Award as it is the only standard available.

---

[15]E.g., good supervision, depending on the postdoc's level of experience and skill, might include guidance in planning a research program, obtaining funding, managing a lab, mentoring others, and finding a permanent position.

[16]The NRC's report *Trends in the Early Careers of Life Scientists* found that life scientists in the 1990s took two years longer to complete a doctorate than their predecessors of the 1960s and 70s.

Further, some federal funding organizations (including NIH) prohibit supplementing a fellowship from other federal grants. The postdocs themselves expressed frustration at having no role in these debates.

In this guide, COSEPUP provides information, principles, and recommendations for all involved in the postdoctoral experience with the goal of enhancing the postdoc experience while preserving the excellence of the research enterprise.

SUMMARY POINTS

➤ Since the 1960s the performance of research, especially in universities, has relied more and more on a growing population of postdoctoral scholars.

➤ The size of the postdoctoral population has increased without a parallel increase in the number of academic faculty positions.

➤ Postdoctoral experience is now seen as a virtual prerequisite for academic careers and many other research positions in the life sciences, physics, chemistry, and some other fields.

➤ The postdocs themselves do not always achieve recognition, status, or compensation commensurate with their experience and skill.

➤ Many postdocs remain in their positions for an indefinite number of years, beyond the five years or so during which they are reasonably considered trainees.

➤ Many postdocs report frustration at not finding the employment positions they anticipated in return for their years of intensive effort.

➤ The demographic characteristics of postdocs are changing. Many postdocs are in their middle to late 30s, with families that include children, and their medical and family support needs have increased.

2

Features of the Postdoctoral Population

Scientists, mathematicians, and engineers seek postdoctoral experience(s) for different reasons. They may be motivated by the desire to deepen their understanding of a field, to learn a new subfield, to switch fields entirely, or to gain experience in an industrial or government facility. Most postdocs share a desire to enter a career that emphasizes long-term research. Some learn that it is possible to combine research expertise with other skills and find rewarding employment in teaching, consulting, business, law, policy making, and other activities. The postdoctoral years are a time to match one's educational background, training, and interests with the changing world of employment and to acquire the skills necessary to enter that world.

The decision (usually made during graduate school) about whether to undertake a postdoctoral appointment is seldom easy and should involve consultation with one's adviser and as many mentors or other experienced contacts as possible. Issues to examine include how much one enjoys doing research, one's level of research skills, and the kind of career that seems most attractive. A postdoctoral experience may raise one's employability, as well as be virtually obligatory in certain fields (notably the biological sciences), but a zest for research should be the first criterion in choosing a postdoc opportunity.

Postdoctoral experiences can differ greatly depending on the disciplines in which they are undertaken, their sources of funding, and the institutional settings in which they occur. The following sections describe those differences in more detail.

21

POSTDOCS IN DIFFERENT DISCIPLINES

Figure 2-1 shows the difference among disciplines in terms of the percentage of doctorates that seek postdoctoral appointments. The percentage is largest in the biological sciences, with physics, chemistry, and the earth sciences not far behind. Differences among disciplines in the median number of years spent in a postdoctoral appointment are discussed in Chapter 1.[1] The early career status of postdocs is illustrated in Figure 2-2, which also shows how employment status varies by field. Figure 2-3 indicates the median postdoctoral salaries. The lowest compensation is provided to academic postdocs in chemistry,[2] the highest to engineering postdocs who work in industry. Table 2-1 compares the number of graduate students in a field with the employment of all doctorates in a field—providing an indication of the likely job market.

The need for postdoctoral study also differs among disciplines. Postdoctoral work is now prerequisite for most long-term employment in the *life sciences*, especially for those planning academic, industrial, or other research careers, as well as teaching careers at many small colleges. In some areas, competition for positions is equally intense at universities and in the private sector, and many life-science PhDs find postdoctoral appointments in biotechnology and pharmaceutical companies. In the *physical sciences* (chemistry and physics), most PhDs who plan research careers are advised to do postdoctoral work. Postdoctoral positions are available at industrial and national facilities, where research facilities are often unique or comparable to those at universities. In *mathematics*, postdoctoral positions are few in number, competitive, and primarily found at universities. Postdocs in mathematics are usually hired as temporary faculty, carry a full teaching load (NSF postdocs teach less), and often have neither a structured research program nor an adviser.

Postdocs are less common among both *engineers* and *social scientists*. As mentioned above, engineers usually enter full-time employment after a master's or bachelor's degree. The number of postdocs in some areas of behavioral and social science (e.g., psychology) has risen recently, primarily in health-related areas.

According to a 1998 survey of four fields by the AAU,[3] the proportion of PhDs accepting or seeking postdoctoral appointments increased from 25 percent in 1975 to over 42 percent in 1995. In biochemistry and physics more than 80

---

[1]As shown in Figure 1-5, biological scientists spend the most years as postdocs, with physicists not far behind.

[2]The low compensation of chemists is due in part to their relatively junior status compared to longer-term postdocs in the biological sciences.

[3]The AAU's Committee on Postdoctoral Education based its 1998 *Report and Recommendations* on "informal" surveys of "selected major research universities" in four disciplines: biochemistry, mathematics, physics, and psychology. The purpose of the surveys was "to gain insight into campus policies and practices governing postdoctoral education and to sample the views of postdocs."

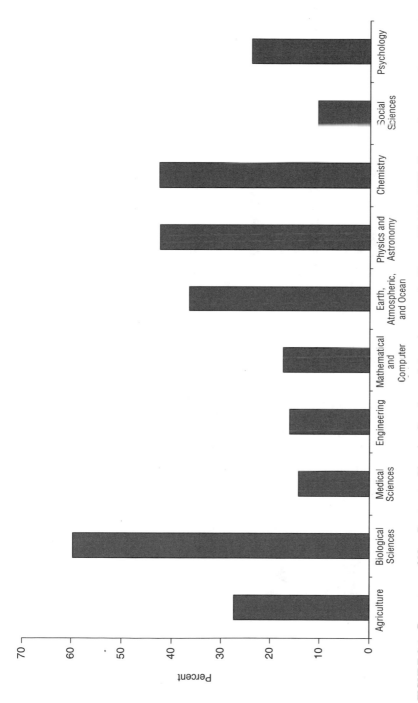

FIGURE 2-1: Percentage of New Doctorates Planning Postdoctoral Appointments, by Degree Field in 1998. Source: Doctorate Records File, 1998.

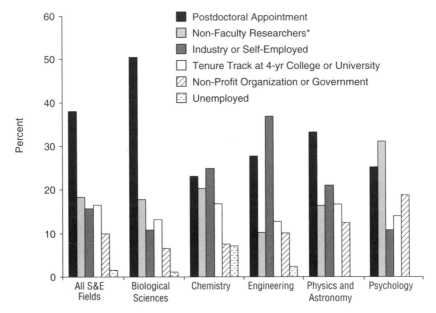

FIGURE 2-2: 1997 Status of 1995 Postdoctorates, by Selected Science and Engineering Field. Source: Merged 1995 and 1997 Survey of Doctorate Recipients.
Note: Non-faculty researchers are full-time academic personnel who do not have faculty rank and indicated their primary work activity is pure or applied research.

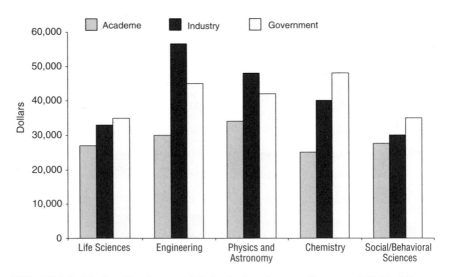

FIGURE 2-3: Median Postdoctoral Salaries by Employment Sector and Field of Doctorate in 1997 for Doctorate in the Six-Year Cohort, 1991-1996. Source: 1997 Survey of Doctorate Recipients.

TABLE 2-1: 1997 Employment Characteristics for All Doctorates and 1998 Graduate Enrollments at Doctoral Granting Institutions

| | 1997 Employment[1] | | | | | | 1998 |
	Total Employed	Academic Faculty*	Tenured & Tenure Track Faculty	Other Academic Personnel	Non-Academic Employment	All Postdoctoral Positions	Full Time Enrollment[2]
Agricultural Sciences	21,264	8,201	7,470	1,448	11,042	573	8,529
Biological Sciences	101,767	41,625	34,640	8,680	39,134	12,328	45,054
Medical Sciences	16,581	7,850	6,390	954	7,276	501	41,019
Engineering	87,954	22,365	20,332	3,205	60,528	1,856	63,806
Mathematics and Computer Science	32,024	17,309	16,012	1,454	12,856	405	26,553
Earth and Atmospheric Sciences	15,766	5,354	4,594	1,578	8,111	723	9,952
Astronomy and Physics	35,803	10,073	8,766	3,130	20,551	2,049	10,326
Chemistry	53,398	12,238	11,016	2,648	36,398	2,114	15,281
Social Sciences	63,116	36,643	33,276	4,915	20,986	572	49,828
Psychology	75,347	21,219	17,790	5,347	46,740	2,041	29,032

* Individuals with faculty rank, tenured positions, or tenure track positions

[1]Source: Survey of Doctorate Recipients, 1997
[2]Source: Survey of Graduate Students and Postdoctorates in Science and Engineering

percent of responding departments said they would not consider hiring a faculty member who lacked postdoctoral experience. A University of California at Berkeley survey that tracked scientists who received PhDs in biochemistry in the 1980s found that 86 percent of them did a postdoc and 40 percent did two or more postdocs with different mentors.[4]

SOURCES OF FUNDING FOR POSTDOCS

Postdocs are paid by a variety of funding sources, and their status as postdocs depends in significant ways on the nature of the source. This status is reflected in differences in pay and other benefits; some postdocs receive no health insurance, for example, while others may receive full health benefits, including dental insurance, sick leave, personal leave, disability, life insurance, and retirement plans.

Within a wide range of variability by field (see Figure 2-4), most postdoctoral researchers are supported on the grant of a PI and may be called *postdoctoral associates* or research associates. A smaller number bring their own funding in the form of fellowships and traineeships, and are often called *postdoctoral fellows*. For example, of the almost 4,500 postdocs supported by the NSF, only about 200 are supported by fellowships.[5] Traineeships also are provided through Center training grants, which are neither PI- nor postdoc-generated. This guide addresses all postdoctoral scientists and engineers, regardless of title or source of funding.

The position of postdocs may differ considerably, according to their source of funding, even though their experiences are identical. Postdocs who work on the grant of a PI are essentially employed to work on the adviser's project and may receive standard benefits from a lab or institution; in some fields, they may also have less flexibility in choosing their research topics and extramural experiences. A postdoc supported by a competitive individual fellowship or grant generally has more prestige and initial flexibility in choosing a program and adviser particularly if the fellow is thereby without cost to the adviser's grants. On the negative side, fellows may not qualify for important institutional benefits. For example, the University of California campuses offer postdocs who are paid from research grants and classified as research associates the same benefits, including vacation, as other employees. By contrast, postdocs who are classified

---

[4]Nerad, M. and Cerny, J. "Postdoctoral patterns, career advancement, and problems," *Science,* 1999, Vol. 285: pp. 1533-5.

[5]Information provided by the NSF to COSEPUP when it held its focus group at NSF indicates that of the 4,478 postdoctoral scholars supported by NSF in 1999, most are in the mathematics and physical sciences (1,885), followed by the biological sciences (1,183), geosciences (452), engineering (339), computer science (265), education and human resources (187), and the social and behavioral sciences (80).

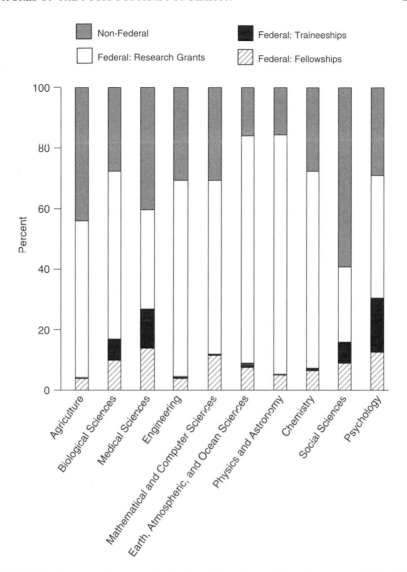

FIGURE 2-4: Source of Support for Academic Postdoctoral Appointees, by Field, 1998.
Source: 1998 Survey of Graduate Student and Postdoctorates in Science and Engineering.

as fellows have no allowance for vacation. Health benefits vary similarly, as indicated by the wide variety of responses to the COSEPUP survey (see Box).

Most individual fellowships are funded by federal agencies, notably the NIH and NSF. Other fellows are supported by foreign governments, private foundations, and private firms. Some fellows receive supplementary funding

Does Your Organization Provide Medical Benefits to All Postdocs and Their Dependents?

This question drew a wide distribution of responses. Among universities, only one-tenth reported paying for medical benefits for all postdocs and their dependents. An equal number provided full medical benefits to all postdocs but not their dependents.

Over one-third of respondents reported that the source of the postdoc's funding determines medical benefit availability. Nearly one-fourth reported that "the organization informs postdocs of medical benefit plans that they and their dependents can enter at their own expense." About one-sixth said that the organization requires postdoc advisers to pay for the medical benefits of their postdocs.

Of nonacademic organizations, more than half reported paying for "medical benefits for all postdocs and their dependents."

COSEPUP Survey Results

when their stipends are insufficient (although there are restrictions on using funds from one federal grant to pay another federal grantee).

Different sources of funding cause some confusion regarding taxes. Institutions tend to regard postdocs who work on research grants as employees, withholding tax money from their pay. Postdocs, however, are not usually regarded as employees for tax purposes; they must file quarterly estimated payments as self-employed individuals. The issue of tax status is a complex one that deserves clarification on the national level,[6] especially with regard to postdocs who are not US citizens.[7]

---

[6]The legal status of postdocs has received limited attention at the federal level, being generally inferred from regulations governing the treatment of graduate students. There is discussion occurring as part of the National Science and Technology Council (NSTC) Presidential Review Directive "Renewing the Federal Government-University Research Partnership for the 21st Century" being developed by the White House Office of Science and Technology Policy and the NSTC. Office of Management and Budget Circular A-21 stipulates that federal agencies can support graduate students as research assistants on federally funded research grants only to the extent that "a bona fide employer-employee relationship" exists between a student and a faculty investigator. There are suggestions that federal policy should be clarified to recognize the dual trainee/employee status of postdocs. For further perspective, see the AAU's "Graduate Education Report: Final Draft," June 12, 1998.

[7]According to numerous COSEPUP interviews with postdocs who are not US citizens or permanent residents, their contributions to the research enterprise are often reduced by their inability to obtain or maintain appropriate visa status. The most common options—the "J" student visa and the "H" professional visa—have substantial drawbacks when applied to postdocs. For example, foreign nationals on a J visa commonly depend on their advisers for visa extensions or conversions to a green card, creating the potential for abuse.

Postdocs in universities may face uncertainties with regard to their funding if they do not know the termination date of the research grant that supports them. Postdocs in government and industrial settings are less often dependent on funding with a fixed termination date and may have fewer financial worries.

POSTDOCS IN DIFFERENT SECTORS

Participants in the COSEPUP focus groups indicated a wide variation in their postdoc experiences according to sector. In industrial and national facilities, postdocs tend to receive higher salaries and clear institutional standing with the same benefit structure as other temporary or contract employees. In universities, stipends are lower, benefits vary by source of funding, and institutional standing may be uncertain.

Postdocs in universities. The vast majority of postdocs work in universities as research associates on PI grants.[8] The exact number of grant-supported postdocs is unclear, however, because different institutions use different titles to describe them, and because major funding agencies (e.g., NSF and NIH) do not have a mechanism for counting or tracking the postdocs they support (though NIH is currently considering a tracking system).

Postdocs in academia have more opportunity than other postdocs to teach and mentor others (especially graduate students). These activities are important in gaining subsequent university employment, and can be essential for landing a faculty position at a four-year college. Most postdocs, however, report little time (or encouragement from advisers) for activities away from research. Without these experiences their job options may be limited (especially for foreign postdocs, many of whom can benefit from stronger language skills). Other critical skills developed by many academic postdocs include writing grant proposals, critically reviewing manuscripts, and presenting research results at disciplinary society meetings.

Although graduate students and postdocs often work closely together in universities, their roles and experiences differ. Graduate students usually have access to special student offices and resources, have many peers, and can rely on oversight from multiple faculty. According to COSEPUP's survey and focus groups, postdocs often work under a single adviser with no other oversight or protection, may have little or no access to institutional facilities or benefits, and sometimes know few or no other postdocs at the institution.

---

[8]Exact proportions are not available. Federal agencies, which support most postdocs via research grants, award grant monies directly to institutions, which may assign various titles to those who are supported by those grants. Thus the same postdoc who is a "research associate" at one institution might be called a "fellow" at another. However, it is clear that the vast majority of postdocs are supported by research grants. As previously stated, of postdocs supported by NSF, some 95 percent are paid from research grants.

The funding situation for postdocs at medical schools has several distinctive features. Many postdocs who plan careers in biomedical research work in medical schools and most are paid from NIH research grants. Clinicians with medical degrees, however, may also do "postdoctoral" research for a year or more without intending a traditional research career. Clinicians who take time away from the hospital continue to be paid a house-staff salary, which is typically more than twice that of most postdocs.

Postdocs in industry. Private firms value postdocs for their up-to-date training and technical skills. Industrial postdoc positions usually differ from academic ones in offering higher salaries, stricter time limits (three years is common), fewer teaching opportunities, and an environment geared toward creating marketable and profitable products.

Practical advantages may include standardized employee benefits, access to well-equipped labs and technology, exposure to industrial culture, teamwork, and management styles, all of which can differ greatly from university life. Depending on the company and research environment, drawbacks may include the chance of being transferred from one's chosen project, limited ability to take ownership of a project, a focus on marketable results, and restrictions on information exchange for proprietary reasons. Restrictions on the use and publication of results may in some cases hinder a postdoc from moving back into academia. Many firms do not hire their own postdocs as staff scientists, or hire only those with specific technical skills.

Postdocs in government facilities. Government postdoc positions, particularly those in large national labs, may offer opportunities not available in a university or industry setting. Some national facilities are unique in the scope of their research, the complexity of their equipment and research facilities, and the size of their research groups.

A national facility may provide a more interdisciplinary setting than a university, as well as more interaction with other divisions and researchers. Some laboratory groups are run collaboratively by staff and postdocs, who jointly make decisions on hiring and other strategies. It is possible for a postdoc to be the only person working on a project, but a team setting is more common.

Like private firms, national facilities afford few teaching or mentoring experiences and may allow a postdoc less flexibility than a university in determining the direction of research. At most national settings, applicants are expected to submit proposals that fit closely with the adviser's ongoing work. Exceptions occur for postdocs who bring their own funding, such as National Research Council (NRC) research associates.

Postdocs at national facilities are usually temporary employees, receiving salaries at the high end of the postdoctoral scale. Terms of two to three years are normal. National labs used to offer postdocs permanent research positions, but this may be less common in times of hiring restraints (some agencies, such as NASA, have imposed multi-year hiring freezes). Some postdocs at government facilities move to "soft-money" grants or contracts, others to jobs in academia or the private sector. Postdocs at some facilities, such as NIH, may be barred from applying for certain fellowships.

Postdocs abroad. Because science is increasingly international, experience in a foreign country can strengthen one's network of potential collaborators and bring valued exposure to different research settings. For the citizens of many countries, postdoctoral work abroad (usually in the US or Europe) is virtually mandatory for an academic career. A smaller number of Americans are willing to seek postdoctoral positions overseas, fearing that too much time "out of sight" can reduce their chances at the best positions at home. For this reason, some overseas postdocs schedule at least one meeting a year in the US. The NSF's International Research Fellow Awards support work abroad, including time for relocating back to the US. The program director reports that few postdocs seek positions abroad, but that those who do have little difficulty finding desirable positions upon their return.

SUB-POPULATIONS OF POSTDOCS

Certain special issues regarding the postdoctoral experience arose repeatedly during focus group and committee discussions: the impact of foreign postdoctoral scholars, challenges to women, and the need for information about minority postdocs. These issues are discussed in more depth below.

Foreign postdocs. The postdoctoral setting is now an international one. For more than a decade, foreign postdocs (i.e., postdocs who are residents of other nations or residents in the US on permanent visas) have played a substantial role in the US postdoctoral experience. At present, slightly more than half of all postdocs in science and engineering are temporary residents (see Figure 2-5). Disciplinary societies and institutions estimate that this percentage holds true for virtually every field in science and engineering.

According to NSF data, about half of foreign postdocs remain in the US after their term's end. The proportion who stay on varies by region of origin; however, postdocs from southeast Asia are more likely to stay than are postdocs from western Europe or Japan, for example. Variations are at least partly attributable to job prospects in their home countries.

US institutions report several concerns over the experiences of foreign postdocs. Many postdocs arriving from abroad have serious difficulties adjusting to the language and customs of this country. Even though lack of language skills has been associated with poor career outcomes,[9] some foreign postdocs—especially those who work with others who speak the same language—do not master English, hampering their teaching and other professional abilities. In addition,

---

[9]"Poor career outcomes" referred to the inability to find a desired position, as reported by Roger Chalkey of Vanderbilt University at the COSEPUP workshop, Dec. 21, 1999.

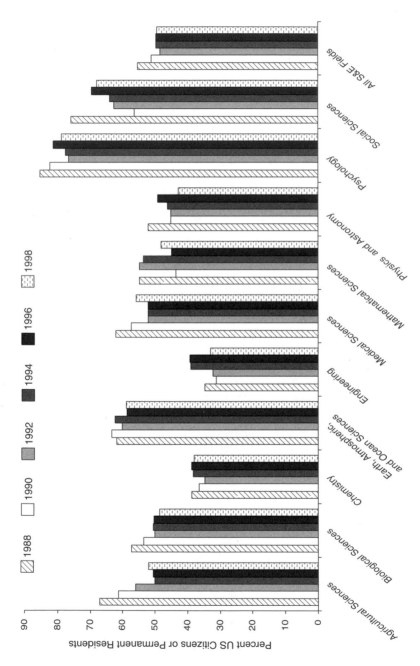

FIGURE 2-5: Percentage, by Field, of US Citizens or Permanent Residents with Postdoctoral Appointments in US Institutions, 1988-1998.
Source: Survey of Graduate Students and Postdoctorates in Science and Engineering.

there is anecdotal evidence that foreign postdocs have received lower compensation than postdocs who are US citizens of the same professional accomplishment.[10] If mentoring problems arise the foreign postdoc is restricted by visa guidelines from changing advisers.

About a third of the institutions responding to the COSEPUP survey did not have staff that dealt specifically with the needs of foreign postdocs. Of those institutions offering help, most found that foreign postdocs needed assistance in the areas of visas, taxes, Social Security, housing, and language skills (see section and COSEPUP Survey Box, "Special Needs of Foreign Nationals," in Chapter 5 for more information).

Women postdocs. The experience of women postdocs differs from that of men in several respects. In some fields, notably engineering and the physical and mathematical sciences, women are significantly under represented as would be expected by their low participation in these fields. Women are outnumbered by men in engineering by more than four to one (826 vs. 205), and in physical and mathematical sciences by a similar difference (3,044 vs. 680). Women postdocs lag behind males in the life sciences (5,920 men vs. 4,363 women) and outnumber men in the social/behavioral sciences (1,173 to 963). Figure 2-6 reflects this same trend when the data is broken down by degree field. Figure 2-7 shows that there is essentially no change in the proportional representation of women as doctorates or postdoctorates. See Appendix Table B-19 for more details.

A second difference can be seen in salary levels (see Figure 2-8). Here women postdocs lag behind their male counterparts in every field. The difference in engineering is most striking, with men receiving an average of $6,000 (20 percent) more, but even in the social/behavior sciences, where women postdocs outnumber men, the "gender bonus" in favor of males is $3,000.

Women in the COSEPUP focus groups reported discrimination against those who take time away from the lab to start a family. Some funding organizations are working on this issue. Burroughs Wellcome now offers flexible timelines on grants for women in the biomedical sciences. (See box on *Postdocs and Family Life*.)

Minority postdocs. Little information is available on members of underrepresented US minority groups who are postdoctoral scholars. (Far more is known about foreign postdocs than minority postdocs.) The available data are provided in Table 2-2. As indicated, in 1997 there were 1,242 minority postdoctoral scholars, or 5.5 percent of the US postdoc population.[11] Their salaries

---

[10]Agencies that compile statistics on postdoc compensation do not distinguish recipients by national status. However, both US and non-US postdocs stated during interviews with COSEPUP that foreign postdocs have received lower compensation than US nationals, and that it has not been uncommon for foreign postdocs (especially women) to work without any compensation.

[11]Survey of Doctorate Recipients, 1997.

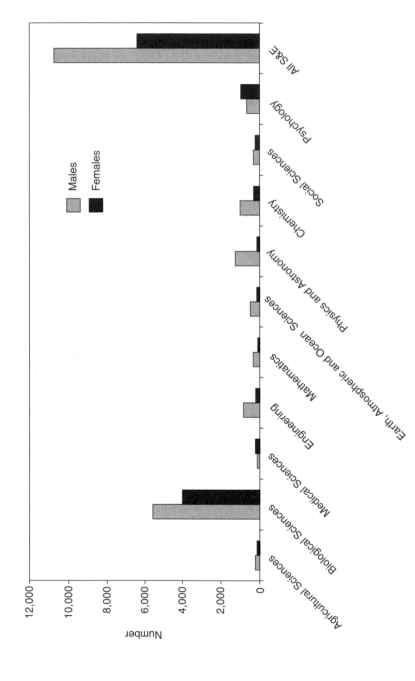

FIGURE 2-6: Number of Male and Female Postdoctorates in 1997, by Degree Field, for the 1991 to 1996 Degree Cohort. Source: 1997 Survey of Doctorate Recipients.

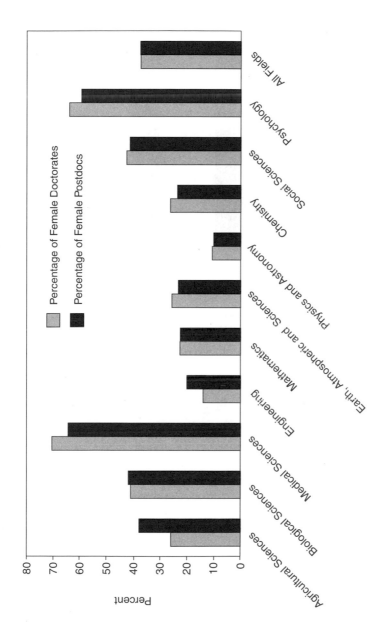

FIGURE 2-7: Percentage of Female Doctorates and Postdoctorates in 1997, by Degree Field, for the 1991 to 1996 Degree Cohort. Source: 1997 Survey of Doctorate Recipients.

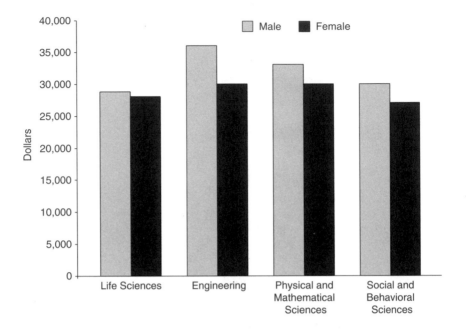

FIGURE 2-8: Postdoctoral Salaries in 1997 for Doctorates in the 1991-1996 Cohort, by Gender and Broad Field. Source: 1997 Survey of Doctorate Recipients.

in academia and industry are $2,000-3,000 higher than those of all postdocs, while their salaries in government are the same. As with all postdocs, the majority are employed in academia.

The latest available data (1997) indicate that members of minority groups are slightly less likely than others to hold postdoctoral positions: 32.3 percent of all PhDs enter postdocs, versus 30.4 percent of minority PhDs. Of those minority group members in regular employment, a greater percentage are employed by universities and four-year colleges than by industry, compared to the rest of the doctoral population. Of all those who received PhDs in 1995 and 1996, 14 percent were employed in universities and four-year colleges and 35.6 percent were employed in industry. For minorities, the picture was reversed: 27.1 percent were employed in universities and 21 percent were employed in industry.

Additional study is needed to gain a better understanding of this key subpopulation and the issues of primary importance to group members. For example, several focus group participants stated that African-American postdocs may

Postdocs and Family Life

Many postdocs have reached an age when they want to start families. Two surveys, at the *University of California at San Francisco* and *Baylor College of Medicine*, indicated that one-third to one-half of postdocs are parents.[12] The Survey of Doctoral Recipients (see Figure 2-9) indicates that more than half of postdocs in all fields except mathematical and computer sciences (45 percent) are married.

Many postdocs report a prejudice among both men and women faculty against women who choose to start a family during postdoctoral training and against men who wish to take parental leave after the birth of a child. Nonetheless, institutions are beginning to create appropriate policies that take family life into consideration. At the *University of Pennsylvania*'s medical school, where the average age of postdocs is 34.5 years, postdocs receive six weeks of paid parental leave. At *Vanderbilt*, women postdocs who have taken time away from a program to have children are allowed to exceed the institution's standard five-year training limit. *The Howard Hughes Medical Institute* builds flexibility into the use of its funding: If a postdoc has a spouse with medical benefits, for example, the postdoc may use the allowance normally allotted to medical insurance for child care.

Useful "survival techniques" reported by postdoc parents include meticulous time management, careful organization of activities (even including "appointments" to spend time with spouses and children), and highly focused attention to each activity. They advise enlisting extra help from family and friends and a clear understanding of parental leave policies. The Survival Skills workshop at the *University of Pittsburgh* notes that the stresses caused by overlapping demands are often associated with depression, and that campus health services usually offer help. *Science*'s *NextWave* web site[13] offers many specific suggestions by postdocs who are parents.

---

[12]See www.bcmitmc.edu/pda/reference/surveyresults.html, www.saa49.ucst.edu/psa/415survey.html
[13]See nextwave.sciencemag.org

Best Practices

find few role models among advisers and may experience even more social isolation than some foreign minorities, who are present in higher numbers.[14]

---

[14]Very few postdocs who are members of underrepresented US minority groups participated in the COSEPUP focus groups, including those held at Howard University and Morehouse University School of Medicine (two of the Historically Black Colleges and Universities, or HBCUs); COSEPUP did conduct additional surveys of minority postdoctoral scholars using e-mail lists, but the response rate was far too low to be generally useful.

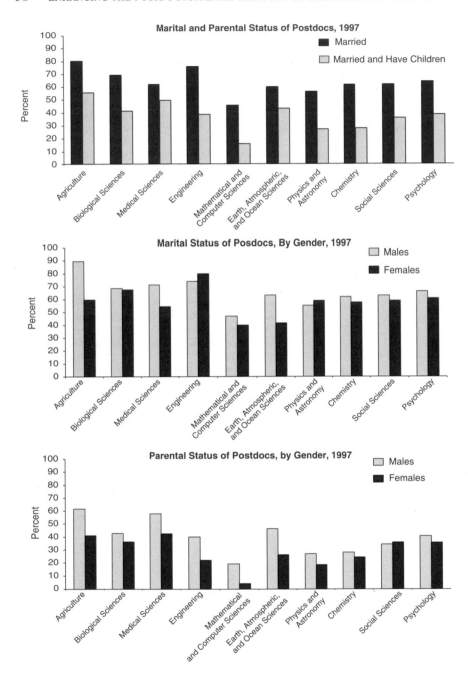

FIGURE 2-9: Percentages of Postdoctorates who are Married or have Children, by PhD Field and Gender, 1997. Source: 1997 Survey of Doctorate Recipients.

TABLE 2-2: Available Data on US Underrepresented Minority Postdoctoral Scholars, 1997. Source: Survey of Doctorate Recipients, 1997.

Number of Underrepresented Minority Postdoctorates by Field

Life Sciences	711
Engineering	79
Math Sciences	60
Physics	22
Chemistry	155
Atmospheric and Geosciences	23
Social/Behavioral Sciences	192
Total	1,242

Median Salaries of Underrepresented Minority Postdoctorates by employment sector

	Industry	Academia	Government
Life Sciences	39,000	30,000	37,000

Number of Underrepresented Minority Postdoctorates by employment sector

	Industry	Academia	Government	Other	Total
All Science and Engineering Fields	75	881	158	128	1,242

Note: Underrepresented minorities are African-Americans, Hispanics, and Native Americans.

Fellowships for Underrepresented Minority Postdocs

While minority graduate students can choose among a variety of special fellowships, minority postdocs have few options. Among them are the following:

The *Ford Foundation Postdoctoral Fellowships for Minorities* are aimed at minority groups "whose underrepresentation in the professorate and in formal programs of postdoctoral study and research in the United States has been long-standing and remains severe as a result of past discrimination." For the year 2001, 25 fellowships of $35,000 will be given for one year of postdoctoral research in fields of science or engineering (excluding "practice-based" professions, such as medicine, law, and social work). Eligible applicants include "current or potential college or university faculty members and researchers" who are U.S. citizens and belong to one of the following groups: African-Americans, American Indians, Alaskan Natives, Native Hawaiians, Native Pacific Islanders, Mexican Americans/Chicanos, and Puerto Ricans. The program is administered by the National Research Council of the National Academies on behalf of the Ford Foundation.

The *UNCF-Merck Postdoctoral Science Research Fellowships* is a program jointly administered by the United Negro College Fund and Merck with ten awards with a stipend of $55,000. This program is "...designed to increase the number of African Americans in the pipeline of biomedical science education and research." The program is open to US citizens who are African Americans. They may work at academic or nonacademic research institutions, but not private industrial labs.

The National Organization for the Professional Advancement of Black Chemists & Chemical Engineers (NOBCChE) Awards, "recognizes outstanding scientists, engineers, and science teachers who have made significant contributions in their fields." While most of their awards are intended for graduate and younger students, the Lloyd Ferguson Young Scientist Award goes to young African American scientists with 8-10 years of professional experience. See also a web site for minority researchers called "Just/Garcia/Hill Science Web Site," at http://hyper.hunter.cuny.edu/jghweb.

Best Practices

SUMMARY POINTS

➤ The postdoctoral years are a time to match one's education, training, and interests with the changing world of employment options and to acquire the skills necessary to enter that world.

➤ A good postdoctoral experience is educational in the sense that it significantly advances one's professional capabilities and increases one's technical abilities.

➤ The postdoctoral experience differs widely according to discipline, sector, and source of funding.

➤ Most postdocs are paid from the grant of a principal investigator and are frequently called research associates. In such situations, they are often treated as employees.

➤ A smaller number of postdocs are paid by external, independent mechanisms (e.g., US fellowships and training grants, foreign government grants). In such cases, they may be classified as students or receive no institutional classification and are called fellows.

➤ "Research associates," "fellows," and postdocs with other titles may all perform the same functions in the same laboratories, and yet their institutional title, tax status, compensation, and benefits may differ in significant and often unintended ways.

➤ The greatest uncertainties and inequities occur in universities, where most postdocs work. In national and industrial facilities, postdocs are usually treated like other temporary or contract employees and receive similar classification, compensation, and benefits.

➤ About half the total US postdoctoral population consists of foreign citizens, half of whom choose to remain in the US after their appointments.

➤ Foreign postdocs face extra challenges in mastering English, adapting to American culture and style of work, achieving equitable compensation, and dealing with visa requirements.

➤ Support mechanisms at host institutions to provide help for foreign postdocs (e.g., with visas, tax laws, and language instruction) are not uniform across the country.

➤ Additional information is needed about postdocs who are members of underrepresented minorities; less is known about these groups than is known about foreign postdocs.

3

Rights, Opportunities, and Responsibilities of the Postdoc

T he fundamental purpose of a postdoctoral experience is to extend and deepen the postdoc's scientific and technical abilities, either in the field of the doctorate or a different field. Because postdoctoral positions seldom require administrative or teaching duties, they provide unique opportunity for researchers to demonstrate originality, creativity, and productivity that will be primary contributors to their future success in research. In particular, postdocs have the opportunity to produce the lead or single author publications by whose quantity and quality they will be judged as they compete for their next professional position.

Responsibility for the postdoctoral experience is shared among the postdoc, adviser, institution, funding organization, and disciplinary societies. This chapter examines the rights, opportunities, and responsibilities of the postdoc, and the importance of postdoctoral activities in shaping a career.

RIGHTS OF A POSTDOC

When an adviser and institution accept a postdoc, that postdoc rightfully expects an experience that provides good training, education, and career enhancement. The following topics were discussed extensively by postdocs and advisers during COSEPUP's focus groups and workshop in an attempt to determine "best practices."

Clear terms of appointment. A postdoc should have a "roadmap" of expectations and goals appropriate to field, sector, and overall career objective. The fundamental requirement is to select an adviser who is an expert and productive

Defining the Postdoctoral Position

Postdocs have sometimes been called the "invisible university." With the rapid growth and importance of the postdoctoral population, some institutions are attempting formal definitions using some or all of these criteria:[1]

- The appointee has received a PhD or doctorate equivalent.[2]
- The appointment is viewed as an apprenticeship—a training or transitional period preparatory to a long-term academic, industrial, governmental, or other full-time research career.
  - The appointment involves full-time research or scholarship.[3]
  - The appointment is temporary.
  - The appointee is expected to publish (and receive credit for) the results of research or other activities performed during the period of the appointment.

---

[1]This definition draws on criteria suggested by the American Association of Universities (AAU, Committee on Postdoctoral Education, *Report and Recommendations,* Washington, DC, March 31, 1998) and by Vanderbilt University School of Medicine (presented by Roger Chalkey at COSEPUP's December 1999 workshop on the postdoctoral experience).
[2]E.g., the MD, DDS, DVM, or other professional degrees in science and engineering.
[3]However, in some disciplines, such as mathematics, the postdoctoral experience commonly includes a major teaching element. Also, some postdoctoral experiences, such as the National Academies' and AAAS Fellowships, introduce the postdoc to the field of public policy.

Practice Description

in the field of the postdoc's interest. Before signing on, the postdoc should gather information that is helpful in evaluating the opportunity: What does the postdoc expect from the experience? What does the adviser expect? (See Box, *Questions to Ask in Choosing an Adviser.*)

Once the postdoc is accepted, an appointment letter or contract should state the basic contractual framework, especially the stipend level, source of stipend, what benefits will or will not be provided (particularly medical), and for how long the grant that supports the postdoc is to be funded. (See Box, *Appointment Letters.*)

The postdoc and adviser should meet early and write down at least a rough research roadmap, including the extent to which the two will collaborate: What are the postdoc's obligations to the lab? How much support and oversight can the postdoc expect? How long should this project take? What are realistic goals: publication? Other benchmarks? How long is funding guaranteed, and how likely is renewal? This exercise is easy to neglect or avoid in the rush of new begin-

Preparing for a Postdoctoral Position

The factors that determine a "good" postdoctoral experience are as various as the personalities involved. But certain key steps deserve careful planning.

Choosing a field. Foremost is the selection of the research area. A post-doctoral research project should be more than an extension of thesis research; it should lead to new skills and a broader outlook. The postdoc should understand in advance what portion of the work is likely to be transportable to his or her next position.

Finding a postdoctoral position. Most postdocs in our focus groups[4] found their positions through personal contacts—advisers, friends, and contacts from professional meetings. Many simply approached potential advisers directly with their qualifications and objectives. Few postdocs are hired after a simple response to ads in journals and on web sites, but such sources provide valuable tips about which institutions are hiring in which fields.

Choosing an adviser. Both experienced postdocs and advisers suggest a thorough investigation before signing on. Some postdocs place paramount importance on the prestige of the principal investigator; others emphasize mentoring ability. A researcher of renown has great power to help—or hinder—a career; a newer assistant professor may offer more attention, responsibilities, and a substantial role in building up a lab. In either case, it is desirable to: 1) arrange a personal meeting and 2) talk with current and former postdocs who have worked with that investigator or organization.

---

[4]Several hundred postdocs, faculty, advisers, administrators, and federal agency staff generously offered their opinions, critiques, and personal experiences at 39 focus groups held around the country.

Practice Description

---

nings. But *clear terms of appointment are essential to prevent later misunderstandings,* and they should be established as early as possible.

Higher compensation. Given the value of postdocs to the research enterprise, one might expect that postdoc salaries would be determined by market forces of supply and demand. The actual situation is somewhat more complex. While some say there is an oversupply of PhDs seeking postdocs, faculty and advisers often perceive difficulty in finding those with the desired skills. Even so, there appears to be little "salary bidding" for the most desirable postdocs, and low compensation is the most vexing issue for many postdocs, especially at universities. Low pay—the salary range for most postdocs is from $27,000 to less than $40,000—is an extra hardship for postdocs with families and those who must begin paying back student loans as soon as they lose their student status. At

---

Questions to Ask in Choosing an Adviser

The best time for a postdoc to evaluate a potential postdoctoral position is before signing on. It is difficult to adjust the major conditions of an appointment once it is underway. Experienced postdocs and advisers suggest the following questions be asked of (and about) a prospective adviser:

1. What are the adviser's expectations of the postdoc?
2. Will the adviser or the postdoc determine the research program?
3. How many postdocs has this adviser had? Where did they go afterward?
4. What do current and past lab members think about their experience?
5. Will the adviser have time for mentoring? Or should I seek out other mentors?
6. How many others (grad students, staff, postdocs) now work for this adviser?
7. How many papers are being published? Where?
8. What is the adviser's policy on travel to meetings? Authorship? Ownership of ideas?
9. Will I have practice in grant writing? Teaching/mentoring? Oral presentations? Review of manuscripts?
10. Can I expect to take part of the project away after the postdoc?
11. How long is financial support guaranteed? On what does renewal depend?
12. Can I count on help in finding a position?
13. Will the adviser have adequate research funds to support the proposed research?

Best Practices

---

the other extreme, a few "award"-level fellowships at national labs pay more than $80,000 a year.

Most salary decisions are made by funding agencies seeking to balance multiple budgetary demands. In 1998, across all fields of science and engineering, the median postdoc salary for recent PhDs was $28,000, half the median salary of recent PhDs in industry and almost one-third less than for PhDs in tenure-track positions.[5] Salaries were even lower before the recent 25 percent increase (effective October 1, 1998) of the National Research Service Award (NRSA) stipend by the NIH, which constitutes a *de facto* standard for much postdoc compensation.[6] Responses to the COSEPUP survey (see Box) indicated that most universities follow the NIH's lead in establishing minimum salaries and yearly increases, with considerable variation, while national facilities tended to have standardized, higher rates than universities, as well as annual increases.

---

[5]NSF *Issue Brief,* December 2, 1998.

[6]Numerous universities and some other institutions where COSEPUP held focus groups cited the NRSA scale in describing their mechanisms for setting postdoc stipends/salaries.

Appointment Letters

By tradition, postdocs have often been invited to work in a researcher's lab with no more formality than a phone call or a handshake. Institutions are now beginning the good practice of issuing a formal letter of appointment that contains important contractual elements. The following model is offered to faculty by the postdoctoral office of one university:

Initial Letter of Appointment Outline

- Offer of postdoctoral position, with brief explanation of research project.
- Effective date of appointment, amount of stipend, source (and expiration date) of funding, and payroll information.
- Length of appointment (e.g., annual, with reappointment contingent on satisfactory performance).
- Leave policy.
- Copy of institutional policies attached with letter.
- Health insurance information and requirements and a description of the other benefits provided and (equally important for the postdoc to know) not provided.
- Intellectual property policy and agreement (enclosed for signature).
- Work eligibility requirements for US citizens and foreign nationals.
- Request for proof of doctoral degree (diploma or registrar statement).
- Request for candidate's signature and return of letter by given date.

Best Practices

About one-third of the respondents said they had no fixed stipend levels because postdocs were paid off grants, because different schools and departments treated them differently, or because stipends were controlled by extramural funding agencies.

Mentoring. In return for working on the adviser's project and with low monetary compensation, the postdoc has the right to expect good mentoring: oversight, feedback, sympathetic consultation, and periodic evaluations. There should be opportunities to present posters and papers and to learn manuscript writing and grant proposal writing. The mentor-trainee relationship can be crucial in helping the postdoc understand the context of his or her research and the requirements of a career focused on advanced research.

The postdoc shares responsibility for making this relationship work, and should understand the multiple demands on the adviser's time. Like any personal relationship, the success of mentoring depends on good will and clear communication by both parties.

Postdoctoral Stipends

Many postdocs, especially in the life sciences, are dissatisfied with the package of compensation and benefits they receive. Stipends vary by a factor of two or more among institutions, some of which have now begun to experiment with more equitable formulas.

The *NIH*, because of its dominance in providing support for postdocs, sets a widely used standard with its *National Research Service Award (NRSA)* scale, whose stipends begin at $26,256 and peak at $41,268 after seven or more years of experience. The scale is not intended to be a model for others, but it has become a *de facto* benchmark for many institutions and funding organizations.

Amid complaints that the NIH scale is unfairly low for experienced researchers, a number of institutions have designed their own standards. The *University of Iowa*, for example, decided to set the salaries of postdocs paid from research grants at twice the graduate student stipend, partly on the basis that postdocs spend all their time on research and a student spends half time. This computes to a salary in the mid-to-upper 30s, and is accompanied by full benefits (except retirement and vacation accrual, which the university plans to include in the future).

The National Institute of Standards and Technology has decided on the standard of the average salary of a land-grant-university assistant professor—now about $50,000—plus $5,500 in travel allowance.

Other institutions have adopted different formulas to supplement stipends that are deemed insufficient. At the *Massachusetts Institute of Technology*, for example, the physics department brings any postdoc stipend up to a minimum of $32,000 to compensate for the cost of living in the Boston area.

The compensation issue has evoked the suggestion that stipends should be increased even if it means reducing the number of postdocs. Officials at the *University of Notre Dame* adopted this strategy for graduate students at the beginning of the 1990s on the premise that "getting better students was more important than getting more students." They increased the undergraduate GPA and total general GRE scores of the graduate students accepted. It was not clear that the strategy reduced the number of applicants accepted, between 1992 and 1999.

It is clear that postdoc compensation is low relative to the compensation of others with comparable skills and education. Postdocs are also entitled to nonmonetary forms of compensation, specifically, to guidance in furthering research and other career skills and in advancing a professional career. For many, these forms of compensation are necessary to a successful postdoctoral experience. Those who do not feel the need for guidance (e.g., people who have been postdocs for five or more years and function essentially independently believe they are already "junior colleagues" of their adviser) often express the greatest displeasure over low stipend levels. (For further discussion of compensation issues, see Levels of Funding in Chapter 6.)

Practice Description

Does Your Organization Establish Minimum and/or Maximum Stipend Levels for Postdocs? If "Yes," Please Specify Dollar Values. If "No," Why Not?

Slightly more than half the organizations answered "yes." Among universities, minimum levels tended to follow the NIH scale (now $26,256 for the first year); a few were lower. At national laboratories and facilities, most salaries began in the $40,000-50,000 range, with lows between $30,000 and $40,000 and a high of $80,000. Some national labs offered "add-on" amounts for "critical skills," from $2,000 to $10,000. In industry, stipends beginning between $30,000 and $40,000 were common.

For "no" responses, institutions listed a range of ambiguities that inhibited the establishment of uniform stipend levels, including the wide variety of job titles and policy differences among departments, schools, or laboratories. Several institutions reported that policies were being prepared.

COSEPUP Survey Results

Multiple mentors. Some advisers who are excellent researchers may have insufficient time or ability to be good mentors. For this reason, several institutions encourage and even require postdocs to seek out multiple mentors or "mentoring committees." The purpose of such committees is not to alter the authority of the PI, but to provide additional perspective and feedback from experienced colleagues. In a broader sense, postdocs can benefit from a diverse community of mentors (representing a range of skills and experience), ranging from peers in the lab to senior investigators in other fields.

Health benefits. Postdocs who are categorized as employees usually have access to insurance and other institutional benefits, such as dental insurance, short-term leave, life insurance, and retirement funds. Problems arise, however, among postdocs who bring their own fellowships, which may or may not include health coverage. This problem is especially troublesome for postdocs with families. Some institutions are setting an example by requiring and/or providing universal access to health insurance for postdocs.

Support in planning a career and finding a job. A postdoc who focuses solely on research may neglect essential steps of career planning. These include acquiring technical and careers skills that will be needed for desired positions, preparing for the next grant or position, publishing results, and building a professional network. Both the adviser and the institution should be sources of assistance in all these areas.

A survey of former postdocs at the University of California at Berkeley indicates that the "best source of job advice" for postdocs in biochemistry and

Is a 'Hot Lab' the Best Lab?

Many graduate students and pre-graduate students assume that a "hot topic" lab is the best lab for postdoctoral work, but hot researchers may or may not provide good mentoring. An indication of effective mentoring may be found in the published record. One mentor advises looking back 10 to 20 years in a major literature database (e.g., Medline for postdocs on the life sciences) and selecting first authors of excellent papers from the lab of the proposed mentor (in most biomedical labs the mentor is the last author). Then fast-forward to the most recent three years and check for citations from the first list of names, especially as first or last author. If the collective first authors of earlier years are producing first-rate, interesting papers today, their previous training may have played an important part. This method is helpful only for evaluating senior mentors; however, for more junior mentors, the best information may come from current and former lab members.

Best Practices

mathematics varies by field (Figure 3-1). For example, postdocs in biochemistry said their mentor was the best source of advice (41 percent), but this was the case for only 15 percent of postdocs in mathematics (who tended to rely on their PhD advisers).[7]

OPPORTUNITIES OF POSTDOCTORAL EXPERIENCE

A postdoc is emerging from the world of students to the broader world of professional research. A postdoctoral apprenticeship offers numerous opportunities to make this transition.

Independence. In graduate school, it is common (though not universally so) for students to work within the structure of the adviser's research program. Many, but not all postdocs work toward greater autonomy and self-direction. Especially in universities and smaller labs outside academia, the goal of the postdoctoral experience may be to become an independent researcher capable of every step of professional research: designing research programs, publishing as senior author, finding grant support for research, and supervising others. These postdocs may have the responsibility for a clearly defined program and work under the supervision of a single adviser. In other kinds of facilities, especially those of industry and government, postdocs may work in teams of dozens or even several hundred

---

[7]Nerad, M. and Cerny, J. "Postdoctoral patterns, career advancement, and problems," *Science,* 1999, Vol. 285: pp. 1533-5.

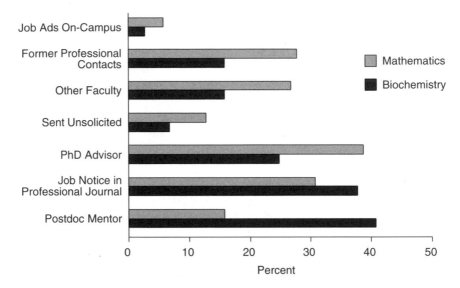

FIGURE 3-1: Best Source of Job Advice for Postdoctorates: Biochemistry & Mathematics. Source: *Science,* 1999, Vol. 285, pp. 1518.

researchers. The goal here may not be to achieve independence in a literal sense, but to mature into interactive and effective team members.

Professional meetings. Most postdocs are aware of the importance of attending professional meetings to network, to present the results of research, and to gain experience in the larger research community. Many postdocs, however, must depend for travel funds on their advisers, whose travel policies vary. Some advisers encourage postdocs to attend meetings; others are reluctant to provide travel funds or allow time for extramural activities. Most postdocs feel the need to attend a minimum of one national meeting a year, preferably two. NIH policy, for example, is to support the travel of its on-campus trainees to one meeting a year, with the opportunity for additional competitive travel awards.

Networking. Professional meetings provide excellent opportunities to meet colleagues and build a professional network of students, other postdocs, and senior researchers. Research communities are relatively small, and meeting one's peers can have lasting importance in finding collaborators for joint projects and contacts who may lead to rewarding employment. For example, the American Chemical Society estimates that 75-85 percent of its members find their jobs through networking.[8] Networking is a process where "more is better," because meeting the right person is often a matter of serendipity.

---

[8]As discussed in the Disciplinary Society Workshop sponsored by COSEPUP and held at the National Academy of Sciences, Washington, DC, January 10, 2000.

RESPONSIBILITIES OF A POSTDOC

Postdocs have dual responsibilities: They must acquire the experiences they need to advance their careers and contribute to the program of their adviser through research accomplishments and interaction with others. Meeting both objectives is most likely when the adviser and postdoc communicate well and share similar expectations.

Career development. Postdocs (with the support of their advisers) must take ownership of their professional development. They need to learn not only the use of new research tools, but also ways to access special resources (such as national and international labs, centers, and multi-user facilities) and to keep up with the exploding streams of scientific communication.

The chances for a satisfying career can be increased through regular attendance at seminars, "getting known" through publications and meeting attendance, course work related to the area of research, integrating research into teaching experiences, developing possible collaborations, and developing skills in grant writing, reviewing, and oral and written communication. This "continuing education" can increase versatility and the chance for a rewarding career.

Intrinsic to "taking ownership" of a career is the element of taking control, of making and seizing opportunities. Timidity is not productive. Rather than waiting for invitations or instructions, successful postdocs ask for what they need, find their own new resources, meet new people, and solicit invitations to speak about their work. Developing a proactive mindset hastens the journey from student to professional. Not all advisers will welcome such initiatives. Their negative reactions can often be ameliorated by improved communication. In very difficult situations, the postdoc may need to consider an alternative situation.

Communicating. Good communication is an essential responsibility of both postdoc and adviser. Postdocs must clearly articulate the skills or training they need; advisers must clearly explain the needs of the laboratory or institution. These needs are most likely to be met if the postdoc steps forward with questions and if the adviser takes the time to listen. The postdoc must also communicate with the institution when help is required.

Contributing to the institution. The more postdocs are able to support the program of their adviser, the greater their value as team members. This can lead to a richer research experience, the respect of other group members, and support in developing a career in the future. In addition to getting the work done, good practices include keeping up with the latest advances, communicating them to others (including the adviser), and interacting regularly with others in both the group and the institution. Expectations about the postdoc's contributions to the immediate community should be discussed carefully with the adviser and other lab members.

Planning for departure. Departure should not be delayed without good reason; the postdoc should neither be pressured to work indefinitely for the adviser, nor become overly comfortable in what should be a finite apprenticeship. If success in the research has proved elusive, the postdoc may be tempted to extend the stay, even indefinitely. This is not always a wise course. These and related issues should be discussed openly between postdoc and adviser from the beginning of the appointment: When should the planning process begin? What are the obligations of adviser and postdoc during and after leaving? Who inherits intellectual property rights—and the project itself—at the point of separation? A good rule of thumb is that the postdoc should begin a systematic job search at least a year before the end of his or her term. In reality, of course, timing is often determined by a job offer. But expectations about departure should be broached and discussed both upon arrival and during periodic evaluations.

SHAPING A CAREER

Academia, government, or the private sector?   The postdoctoral tradition began in universities. Many faculty still place the highest value on careers in academia, and assume that their postdocs will follow them there.

Nonacademic careers, however, are both more common and more acceptable than in the past. In some fields (such as biotechnology, computer science, and electrical engineering), postdocs value nonacademic positions as highly as academic jobs. Even so, many postdocs lack up-to-date information about research careers. In a 1999 survey of junior scientists at the University of California at Berkeley, 55 percent of respondents said their advisers encouraged them to pursue academic jobs, but fewer than 1 percent were advised to obtain positions in industry, government, or the non-profit sector.[9] A second 1999 survey of postdocs at Berkeley indicated that the number anticipating careers as "a professor with an emphasis on research" had dropped from 69 to 59 percent since the beginning of their postdoctoral experience. Instead, they cited the goals of "research in industry or national lab," "consultant," or "start their own company." The leading reasons given for this change were "difficulty obtaining an academic job" and "money."[10]

The first Berkeley survey noted a wide difference in salaries for academic and nonacademic positions. About half of the cohort of biochemists who earned PhDs in 1982-1985 were working outside academia in 1995. This group earned almost $22,000 more in median annual total salary (including all income sources) than those employed in the academic sector, where the median salary was $57,000.

---

[9]Nerad, M. and Cerny, J. *PhDs–Ten Years Later,* a national study funded by the Mellon Foundation, 1999, with selected analysis funded by the NSF. A report on the study has been published in *Science* (cited above).

[10]McPheron, L. and Nerad, M. "Results of a Survey of Postdoctoral Appointees at UC Berkeley," University of California at Berkeley (mcpheron@nature.berkeley.edu), 1999.

Developing career skills. Once a postdoc can see the outline of a career, gaining the right skills can be the key to expanding choices and finding the right position. These skills include such general abilities as clear writing, public speaking, leadership, teamwork, teaching, and mentoring. Given the competition for research positions, experience in teaching can be a strong advantage, especially for academic employment. Teaching experience also prepares the postdoc to communicate with people who work outside research or specialize in other fields.

Job hunting. The job search usually begins with help from the adviser, whose professional contacts are invaluable. However, postdocs should also develop their own network of contacts. One adviser suggests: "Let your presence be known in the field; be as public as you can. Departmental meetings, professional meetings—take advantage of those ten minutes in the sun." The search must be tailored to the desired sector. For example, teaching experience will be more valuable in an academic setting; an industry employer is likely to require evidence of good communication and team skills.

Career expectations and reality. The 1998 AAU study reported that two-thirds of postdocs expected to find a tenure-track position at a research university, but that only about one-fourth of "recent postdocs" had done so. (An additional one-fourth went to another postdoc and 10 percent went to non-tenure-track (but somewhat more regular than a postdoc) positions such as fellow, research assistant, and adjunct instructor.) A 10-year follow-up study of 23 PhD graduates from the 1987 class of the M.D. Anderson Cancer Center in Houston showed similar results. Sixteen had permanent jobs, but only 10 were in research, with only five of those in tenure-track positions. Seven were still in postdoc positions a decade later.[11]

---

[11]Bunk, S. *The Scientist*, 1998, Vol.12, 1, p.1.

SUMMARY POINTS

➤ Postdocs should have the opportunity to enhance their research experience, become independent researchers, become known through publishing and presenting their results at professional meetings, and advance their careers by networking with colleagues.

➤ They have the right to clear terms of appointment, appropriate compensation and benefits, serious mentoring, and support in career planning and finding a regular position.

➤ Postdocs have dual responsibilities: 1) to acquire the experiences they need to advance their careers, and 2) to contribute to the program through research accomplishments, personal growth, and interaction with others.

➤ Postdocs share the responsibility with their adviser of communicating well regarding their progress and expectations.

➤ In planning careers, more postdocs are finding opportunities in non-academic positions, but they must take the initiative to learn about acquiring the skills needed to qualify for entrance to growing employment areas, often outside their specialty.

➤ Some women postdocs face special problems because of their gender, and have great difficulty in taking time to start a family.

➤ Gaining the right skills can make a large difference in finding rewarding positions and expanding career choices. These include general abilities such as clear writing, public speaking, leadership, teamwork, computer skills, teaching, and mentoring.

A Successful Postdoctoral Experience

The elements of a successful postdoctoral appointment are as variable as the postdoctoral population. For one unabashedly upbeat postdoc on a laboratory fellowship (we'll call her Sue), these elements included early preparation, supportive colleagues, a fascinating research topic, the opportunity to learn time management and self-reliance, and an effective—though somewhat distant—mentor.

• *Early preparation*: Even as a graduate student in geochemistry, Sue began building ties to the research group where she wanted to go as a postdoc. "To get the most out of an experience, you have to offer something. I did my graduate work in geochemistry; I wanted to work with a group in planetary physics, and I was able to show them that I had something to contribute. I began doing some projects with them while I was in graduate school, so the transition was relatively smooth. One of the best reasons to do a postdoc is to learn a new field, but it's best to prepare the ground early."

• *Supportive colleagues*: "I didn't always know where I was going, but it was fairly easy to seek out good advice and constructive criticism both in my own institution and elsewhere. A big challenge, and a difference from graduate school, is that you've got to start putting together your own professional network of collaborators and friends with whom you're going to be building your career. It's a good habit to spend time every week meeting new people, networking, looking at people who are successful to see how they do it."

• *A topic of interest*: "I loved my work, and this is one reason it was successful. I published 12 or 13 papers during three years as a postdoc, including one in *Science*. I got to work on a variety of problems without getting stuck in something too narrow. I was fortunate enough to have a great deal of freedom. I could follow my curiosity, and that allowed me to be very productive. I had the opportunity to propose my own research and get it funded."

• *Learning self-reliance*: "I spun my wheels for the first few months, trying to figure out what to do first, but there were some advantages to that experience. If you're going to be an independent researcher, sooner or later you've got to learn to fly the plane. When I was a grad student, I used to do all my own instrument work, because my time was cheap and there wasn't anyone else to do it. When I became a postdoc, I was paid more and I had technical staff. I had a big adjustment in mindset about organizing better and making the wisest investments of my time."

• *Effective mentoring*: "I saw my adviser several times a week. He wasn't very involved with my research, but what he did was right for me. He was always supportive, gave me a long leash, and made sure I got to give talks at important conferences. He did this for all his postdocs—made sure that certain doors were unlocked. What you do with that advantage, once you go in that door, is your business. Again, you're the one who's going to fly the plane. In the end, I was fortunate enough to be hired by the same institution where I did my postdoc."

Profile

A Difficult Postdoctoral Experience

Joe, who has had two postdoctoral appointments in academic environments and now works in the biotechnology industry, says it can sometimes be difficult to anticipate—or prevent—a frustrating experience. For his first postdoc, he carefully chose an adviser whose project in the life sciences seemed to fit nicely with his own interests, but a series of difficulties blunted his productivity. He offers a summary of his experience, and some lessons he learned:

- *Know when to cut your losses:* In his first year, Joe tried several experimental approaches that failed to give results. His adviser was seldom in the lab to offer guidance, and Joe was slow to change direction. When he tried to consult other senior scientists, his adviser refused to allow it. "She felt this was interfering with her laboratory. In retrospect, I probably should have cut my losses and moved on. But there's great pressure to keep going, to tough it out."
- *Understand your adviser's policy on publication:* In his third year, Joe had finally found a promising new direction, obtained results, and written them up for publication. His adviser, however, did not allow him to send out the paper because she felt it should be a "bigger story." "The timing was critical for me. I had to be applying for jobs, and I had no publications. I was ready to have my work judged by my peers, and I was unable to do so. She finally rewrote and published the paper—after I'd left the lab."
- *Talk with former lab members before signing on:* Joe talked only with current lab members, who he now knows are not in a position to be critical. Later he learned that he was the fifth postdoc to leave that particular lab without publications or jobs. "I should have talked with some former members, because they are freer to be honest. In a good training environment, postdocs are getting jobs and continuing their research. I might have saved myself a lot of difficulty."
- *Be clear about your agenda:* He went on to do a second postdoc, with better—defined goals. "I needed publications, and I was frank about this with my second adviser. That lab was doing work in my field. I was offered a year's support, and after that I knew I would be on my own. It was a fair offer, and clear. After nine months I was able to raise my own funding. I got my publications, the work came out well, and I entered the job market in good shape."

Profile

4

The Postdoc and the Adviser

The need for effective supervision of junior researchers does not end with the PhD. Those who move from graduate school to postdoctoral appoint-ments stand to benefit greatly from the contributions of their advisers. Many advisers do an excellent, careful, and conscientious job of assisting with the professional development of their postdocs. However, some let other tasks of the research enterprise outweigh their mentoring duties.

THE ADVISER AS MENTOR

When advisers become effective mentors and assume responsibility for guiding, challenging, and championing their postdocs, they can have a powerful and enduring effect on the careers of these junior investigators. At the same time, responsive postdocs can advance their own and their advisers' careers and become valued colleagues and collaborators after completion of the postdoctoral appointment.

Creating a productive mentoring relationship takes considerable time and effort on both sides, however, it is important for advisers and postdocs alike to appreciate its unique tensions and potential benefits. The tensions are, to some extent, built in: The investigator's lack of time or inclination for mentoring leaves ample room for misunderstandings or neglect. Luckily for the relationship, the benefits are largely inherent as well. The postdoc is motivated to exchange skills and hard work for guidance and entrée to a professional world.

Benefits for the adviser. The nature of the mentoring relationship becomes clearer if one takes a closer look at its potential benefits. The adviser stands to

Communicating with the Postdoc

Susan has spent nearly two years exploring the research problem she chose before beginning her postdoc. She has one more year before expiration of the grant that supports her work. She has gained a thorough understanding of her problem, but the facts she has gathered do not support the working hypothesis of the lab. With time growing short, she is reluctant to admit her uncertainty to her adviser.

Comment: An alert adviser would be aware of Susan's findings and initiate discussions with her, inviting her to a strategy session. The adviser has already learned, probably through hard personal experience, that research seldom follows a straight line. Good communication and mutual trust can allow the adviser to undertake an honest appraisal of both Susan's work and the other work in the lab in order to decide whether or not the working hypothesis requires modification.

Best Practice Scenario

gain from the training, energy, and enthusiasm of the postdoc, who makes it possible for the adviser's research program to advance. Many postdocs arrive in their new positions as accomplished researchers; attentive advisers have already ensured (to the degree possible) that the interests of the postdoctoral candidate fit well with their own and those of the research group. When the fit is good, it is common for advisers to count on their postdocs to bring the latest skills and knowledge to the lab. Advisers who are good mentors can benefit by attracting the best postdocs on the basis of their reputation as mentors.

The adviser also benefits in less tangible ways. Simply put, it is personally and professionally gratifying to teach others what one has learned and to help them advance toward fulfilling careers.

Benefits for the postdoc.   From the postdoc's point of view, advisers can contribute to a varied learning experience that comprises many kinds of skills in addition to technical ones: developing a plan of research, managing time, supervising students and technicians, overall lab management, deciding when and where to publish, creating a network of professional contacts, acquiring "career" skills (such as communication and teamwork), understanding ethical and proprietary issues, and, eventually, finding a regular job.

In a broader sense, the adviser can contribute perspectives that can be gained only from professional experience: how to avoid investigative dead ends; how to build a research project that will contribute to the postdoc's career, the adviser's program, and the research enterprise as a whole; and how to know when a project is near completion. All these contributions, like those of the postdoc, are most rewarding for both parties when the activities of postdoc and adviser are complementary.

Adding New Research Tools

After completing his PhD in computational mathematics, Steven was admitted to a prestigious new program in bioinformatics at a university. He had never formally studied the life sciences, but he was assured that his contribution would be welcome because of his strength in mathematics. After six months in his new position, however, he was frustrated by his inability to follow the reasoning of his biological colleagues. His adviser sensed Steven's frustration and suggested a one-semester immersion in selected biology courses. After some hesitation, because of fear of harming his standing with the group, Steven accepted the advice, and later rejoined the group with renewed confidence.

Comment: *Much exciting research takes place at the intersections of disciplines, but interdisciplinary work places heavy demands on researchers on both "sides" of an intersection. More than superficial knowledge of the complementary field may be required for productive collaboration. A flexible adviser may find that encouraging additional study for certain postdocs can advance both the postdoc's work and the adviser's program.*

Best Practice Scenario

RESPONSIBILITIES OF THE ADVISER

The adviser's overall responsibility is to help advance the postdoc's scientific abilities and professional career. The adviser who regards a postdoc as a colleague-in-the-making will gain in productivity and rise in the estimation of other researchers.

First steps. The first task is to deliberate carefully before inviting a postdoc to join a program. What is this person's potential for making important contributions to research, both as a scholar and as a member of the lab or research team? How well might his or her particular skills fit strategically within the organization? Although these questions can seldom be answered with certainty, the adviser who seeks references and a face-to-face meeting has a better chance of making a match that benefits both the program and the postdoc.

At the beginning of an appointment, most postdocs benefit from trying to develop a "training plan" that is adapted to the activities of the adviser or laboratory. The attempt may or may not succeed at the outset, but it serves the purposes of stimulating early communication, teaching the importance of thinking strategically, and moving the postdoc forward. Laying out research objectives should be a mutual responsibility until the postdoc is ready to conceive, plan, and execute his or her own research project.

Selecting a research problem. The adviser can help frame a good problem in several ways. Most important, the postdoc must care deeply about it—and this enthusiasm must be shared by the adviser. Second, the problem must be important for the field as well as for the postdoc's career. Third, approaching a good problem can stimulate the postdoc to understand how to convert initial questions into a working hypothesis and to understand the magnitude of resources (time, equipment, expertise, and money) needed to accomplish the work. Early discussions should include the extent to which the postdoc can expect to take ownership of a project and plan on continuing the research after the postdoctoral appointment.

Evaluating a research problem can also be illuminated by what Nobel Prize winner Herbert Simon of Carnegie Mellon University calls a "secret weapon"— a feature that will allow the postdoc to accomplish something that others have not yet been able to accomplish. This special advantage may be a new method, piece of equipment, or reagent; a special insight (i.e., an insight made possible by an unusual background); a talented team; or even a willingness to devote an extraordinary amount of time to the work.[1]

Research guidance. In return for the postdoc's contributions, the attentive adviser will guide the postdoc toward becoming a better researcher. Most postdocs need such guidance especially in the early months to avoid wasting time. They don't, however, need micromanaging; the adviser's goal is to allow the postdoc to grow toward independence and a relationship that becomes a collaborative one.

As postdocs gain independence, they need to learn, under the mentor's guidance, to manage their time and often the time of technicians. They benefit from reading deeply and broadening their intellectual portfolio. They must learn to answer important questions: What distinguishes an important research problem from a routine one? What strategies are most likely to succeed? How much time will be needed to answer a question? People who lack the time or inclination to provide an educational experience should not accept the responsibility of mentoring postdocs.

Some of the adviser's most important contributions may be to set the research framework: to introduce the postdoc to potential collaborators and influential colleagues, ensure that the postdoc has adequate resources for the research program, and advise against being trapped in a narrow or unpromising line of work. As work progresses, some postdocs may put off publishing their work inappropriately because of their desire to produce a prize-winning paper or "perfect" experiment. Advisers can help by reviewing and discussing the work and urging the postdoc toward publication. They should also take meticulous care to give the postdoc proper credit for authorship, seminars, disciplinary society presentations, and other achievements.

---

[1] For Professor Simon's lecture, see the University of Pittsburgh survival skills site, www.edc.gsph.pitt.edu/survival/.

Learning to Collaborate

Lee is a brilliant but shy student who earned a postdoctoral appointment in chemistry at a research university. Her strengths at the bench were undeniable, and she quickly won the confidence of her adviser. After two years of work, however, Lee had made few friends outside the lab, and her work was progressing more slowly than expected. Her adviser surprised Lee by asking her to mentor two graduate students who had just joined the lab. Lee balked at this request, but the adviser insisted. The adviser also paid for Lee's travel to a professional meeting and arranged for her to present a poster. Several months later, Lee formed a small journal club around the two students; a month after that, she began a research collaboration with a postdoc she met at the meeting.

Comment: *Research is increasingly collaborative, and the performance of successful research depends heavily on interacting with others. The adviser had the wisdom to see that Lee was blocked by her reticence and to insist (at the risk of jeopardizing her good relationship with Lee) that she begin to develop contacts and activities outside the lab.*

Best Practice Scenario

Advancing the career. In addition to guiding the postdoc in research skills, the adviser can help the postdoc identify and acquire necessary career skills, such as those of communication, publication, grant writing, and management. Those who aim for professorships, independent research, or research management must be assisted and challenged in appropriate, educational ways. Some postdocs may prefer to continue their research careers in valuable supporting roles, such as that of a research scientist working as a member of a team on their own or the research grants of PIs.

Attending professional meetings is one of the most important ways a postdoc can enhance professional visibility, gain confidence, and build a network of contacts. An adviser can save time and share power with postdocs by asking them to present research results at meetings. Even when there is no paper to present, a postdoc should attend one or two professional-society meetings or workshops a year, with financial help from the adviser when necessary. Many postdocs hesitate to ask about attending meetings if they lack designated travel funds or find that activities outside the lab are discouraged.

Postdocs need practice and coaching in writing grant proposals, supervising others, teaching, making spending decisions, creating a budget, and reviewing papers. Encouraging single or lead-author publications by postdocs is an important aspect of mentoring. When postdocs acquire such skills, they are better equipped to contribute to the program and to compete for future positions.

Knowing When to Suggest a Change

Dr. Brown accepted Carl for a postdoctoral appointment in his theoretical physics group after a telephoned recommendation from a colleague and a brief meeting with Carl. He was impressed by Carl's enthusiasm for physics and his eloquence in describing several goals in cosmology. After a few months of work, it was apparent that Carl enjoyed his work and was progressing. He requested time to teach an undergraduate course as well. Dr. Brown agreed with some reluctance, needing all the help he could get with the research lab. At his year-end review, Carl told Dr. Brown that he enjoyed his teaching as much as his research, and hoped to make teaching a major emphasis in his career. Dr. Brown suggested a minor course change toward a career at a four-year teaching college.

Comment: This turned out to be a good move. Carl could continue his research and teach in an environment where both activities were valued. Through good communication, Carl was able to express his preference to an adviser for whom teaching was not the first priority, and the adviser had the sensitivity to see that Carl's talents could be more fully applied in a different kind of career. Advisers must often base their acceptance of a postdoc on a brief impression or the opinion of others. Mismatches do occur, and although they may be painful to acknowledge, the best course of action may involve a change. More painful is the potential waste of productive years, which for some PhDs are better spent in non-research activities.

Best Practice Scenario

Balancing the needs of the program and the needs of the postdoc. Laboratories and research groups need continuity and a "critical mass" of expertise (including postdocs) to complete major projects, and postdocs need the freedom to find their own challenges. A postdoc is in the lab not only to make valuable scientific contributions but also to expand his or her accomplishments. A mentor has the responsibility to help the postdoc see a project (or aspect of the project) to completion in a reasonable time (usually not more than five years). Future employers will want to see evidence of perseverance and an ability to attain successful closure on research problems.

Mentoring. Advisers can enhance the training of postdocs in both explicit and implicit ways, such as modeling good practices of research, leadership, and ethical conduct. Advisers who are too busy to fulfill mentoring duties can bring in help (such as a mentoring committee) or orient the postdoc toward institutional or other resources.

Flexibility. It is common for research goals to change as postdocs mature. It isn't always easy for a program to adapt, but flexibility on the part of the adviser may lead to great rewards in the form of the postdoc's growth and contributions.

Mentoring

When the *J. David Gladstone Institutes* in San Francisco wanted to ensure that its 60 postdoctoral scholars were receiving adequate mentoring, the administration undertook a year-long study, with the following results:

- Discussions of mentorship have become part of the annual performance reviews for fellows and PIs.
- Postdocs are surveyed annually on the mentoring they receive, and confidential results are sent to the PI, the director, and the human resources office.
- PIs receive additional training in mentoring.
- A Women in Science Program was established to assist women postdocs.
- Trainees were made aware of existing procedures for addressing problems between the postdoc and the mentor.
- PIs are required to discuss career plans and prospects with postdocs at least yearly.
- Human resources will provide all postdocs with both a letter of appointment and a letter of completion.

At the *University of Pittsburgh*, one department requires each postdoc to select a small faculty "mentoring committee" for informal meetings and guidance. Postdocs are encouraged to choose "potential role models" as committee members. One postdoc reported after her first meeting, "It was the best meeting I ever had. I didn't feel like the trainee; I was just talking to three other researchers. They were at opposite ends of my project and brought different perspectives."

At *Albert Einstein College of Medicine*, one department finds that effective mentoring can be accomplished through weekly work-in-progress groups. "Each postdoc has to present their research once a year," says a dean. "Everyone knows where they stand. If a person is foundering, the group will get together at other times to advise."

At *Eli Lilly and Co.*, mentoring of its 75 postdocs is done both by the Science Advisory Council and by individual "research advisers." The Advisory Council, which oversees the scientific integrity of the program, meets with a postdoc at least once during their tenure—usually at the midpoint. These meetings give postdocs the opportunity to showcase their work for senior management, build their network of contacts, and work on getting sponsorship. Postdocs also meet regularly with their research adviser. The position of research adviser is prestigious; before advising a postdoc, a researcher must demonstrate success at mentoring technicians.

At *Johns Hopkins School of Medicine*, mentors are asked to perform a formal review of each postdoc's progress at least twice a year. A written record of the review should indicate progress and next steps to be taken.

Best Practices

Many postdocs (and students) will work most effectively when they are encouraged to pursue some of their own ideas. As one faculty adviser has said, "When you are a good mentor, people are happy; the work gets done." On a larger scale, the mentor should also be flexible when the career goals of the postdoc change.

Communication. Frequent communication helps prevent problems from growing into grievances. Patience is required, as well as discernment: One postdoc might need regular, detailed instructions; another might need only to hear, "Do what excites you."

Good communication is a mutual responsibility. Postdocs and advisers alike must have the courage to raise uncomfortable issues. Regular weekly or biweekly meetings can help maintain communication. Meetings and other forms of communication are indispensable in establishing and maintaining the foundation for a mentoring relationship. It is likely that breakdowns in communication are at some level the causes of most personal problems that occur in the research environment.

In one lab, for example, the adviser holds an annual meeting with all lab members. For the meetings, member are asked to write out both their long-term career goals and their goals for the coming year. Discussion of these goals facilitates ongoing communication among members.

Honest evaluations. Many postdocs, especially in universities, express concern that they seldom or never receive formal evaluations. Half the institutions responding to the COSEPUP survey required "no official performance reviews of any type" (see Box).

Evaluations need not be time-consuming. Brief, regular meetings can form a basis for useful feedback, suggestions for improvement, and performance assess-

---

Does the Organization Require Performance Evaluations Throughout a Postdoc's Appointment?

Of academic institutions, the largest number (47 percent) reported that "no official performance reviews of any type are required." Only 17 percent required them, and 13 percent reported that "Documented progress reviews are performed by the respective adviser at his/her discretion."

By contrast, the majority (70 percent) of nonacademic institutions required regular performance evaluations.

In the "other" responses, some respondents indicated that they are examining and/or revising their policies on evaluations. Others described optional or discretionary approaches ("Depends on program"; "Depends on funding source"; "Varies by unit"). Several institutions expected the adviser to take responsibility for any evaluation, without formal reporting to the institution.

COSEPUP Survey Results

ments. But written progress reports (for example after the first 6 months and then annually) are needed to clarify performance for the postdoc, the institution, the funding organization, and potential employers. A record of evaluations is especially important if they are needed for reappointment or to find another job.

Evaluations are useful only if they are honest. Good work should be acknowledged and rewarded; less-than-good work should receive equally frank appraisal. When a postdoc lacks the necessary aptitude for a career of research, the adviser must say so. No one's interests are served by allowing a subpar performance to continue indefinitely only to avoid an unwelcome evaluation. On the other hand, evaluations should be constructive, not punitive. The objective of regular evaluation is to identify weaknesses or problems, to create plans to address them, and ultimately to raise the level of performance and eventually the success of the individual.

Ethical and proprietary issues. The adviser should take the lead in discussing ethical standards early and often, especially with new postdocs and with postdocs from countries where standards may differ. Authorship especially carries a great potential for misunderstandings. A good policy is for the adviser and postdoc to discuss authorship policy early. Of course, no policy can cover all contingencies. A designated lead postdoc, for example, might lose interest or shift to another project.

Other issues that should be discussed include plagiarism, public presentation of results, and the integrity of data. For example, several postdocs in focus groups reported being asked not to publish results that did not agree with the adviser's work; this request is not acceptable. Such issues underline the need for good communication and mutual trust.

Every person supported on a federal training grant is required to receive instruction in research ethics. Given the importance of responsible conduct to both the research enterprise and the careers of individual researchers, a mentor should ensure that postdocs are instructed about any ethical issues of relevance to a particular program. Such issues may include data management, the use of human subjects, experiments on animals, conflicts of interest, resolving ethical dilemmas, whistle blowing, and handling research sponsored by a for-profit entity.[2]

Resolving disputes. Because of their position of power, advisers have the larger responsibility in resolving disputes, especially if the postdoc is directly supported on a research grant. Frequent, open communication can prevent misunderstandings. When an impasse develops, the adviser (or postdoc) should not hesitate to ask an ombudsperson or other neutral party to discuss the issue. (See also *The role of the ombudsperson* in Chapter 5.)

---

[2]For further discussion of ethical issues, see the National Academies' publication, *On Being a Scientist: Responsible Conduct in Research, 1995,* available via the Academies' web site and also through the National Academy Press at www.nap.edu.

Poor Advising Practices

The following true examples, described by postdocs and advisers during the committee's focus groups, illustrate situations or behaviors that can damage not only a postdoc's experience but also the morale and accomplishments of a program.

- *At a professional society meeting, a postdoc met several colleagues from other institutions who were engaged in the same field of research. They invited her to participate in a collaborative project involving an aspect of her lab's research. When the postdoc asked permission, her adviser refused on the grounds that revealing the details of the lab's work might give others an advantage.*

Comment: Scientific research is increasingly collaborative. A postdoc should be encouraged to develop her professional network and to seek out cooperative projects.

- *An adviser who was a renowned lab director declined a postdoc's offer to help assemble the lab's grant proposal. "That's my responsibility," he said.*

Comment: Grant writing is a skill most postdocs need to acquire. While a major grant is indeed the PIs responsibility, the postdoc also needs to learn that skill. The postdoc should be asked to write the portion of the grant that describes his or her own work.

- *An adviser with a wide reputation for hard work informed his group of postdocs that they could take a total of 12 days off each year, and that otherwise they were expected to be in the lab every day, including weekends.*

Comment: Advisers, following institutional policies, should establish reasonable policies for time off.

- *A postdoc whose adviser was rarely in the lab felt the need for more supervision while learning a new field. When he asked the adviser's permission to find an additional mentor, she refused on the grounds that another person would be intrusive and would jeopardize the advising relationship.*

Comment: The adviser does not "own" the postdoc, who can often benefit from multiple mentors—especially if the primary adviser is often unavailable.

- *A foreign postdoc, after working in a program for several months, wanted to return home for Christmas vacation with his family. When he inquired about leave policy, he was told that his institution did not provide vacations for postdocs and that his adviser expected him to be in the lab year-round.*

Comment: Minimum vacation benefits for postdocs should be set by institutions and these policies should reflect the benefits accorded to other members of the lab or program.

Practice Description

Turning Research into Manuscripts

After two productive years as a postdoc at a national laboratory, Paul had gathered an impressive body of data on climate change resulting from the eruption of an ancient volcano. His well-planned fieldwork had led to numerous poster sessions and several hundred pages of unpublished notes, but no publications. When his adviser urged him to publish, Paul responded that he needed a few more data points. After a more extended talk, the adviser learned that Paul, despite his excellent work, was inhibited by the recent work of a competitor, whom he was determined to "blow out of the water."

Comment: *The adviser persuaded Paul to begin publishing after explaining that 1) research accomplishments usually occur in small steps, 2) the feedback from his colleagues after publication is essential to further steps, and 3) his career would stall unless he communicated his work in public. Few junior investigators have a basis for understanding when and how much to publish; they need the advice of experienced mentors.*

Best Practice Scenario

The productivity of a lab depends not only on the research skills of the adviser, but also on his or her ability to urge the postdocs, grad students, technicians, and other researchers toward an ethic of collaboration. Discord or feuding among lab members can be as destructive to a postdoc's experience as a poor-mentoring relationship. Foreign postdocs may suffer disproportionately from lab disputes, especially if they depend on their adviser to maintain their visa status.

Finding a regular job. The adviser is usually the person best situated to help the postdoc move to the next position. The quality of that position reflects not only on the postdoc's personal abilities, but also the quality of the program and the mentoring ability of the adviser. Traditionally, advisers in universities have expected their postdocs to move to the kinds of academic research positions that they themselves held. Today, informed advisers know that many more postdocs than formerly will move to the private sector or government, where employers may require a slightly different set of skills—in particular, a variety of personal skills, such as abilities in teamwork, communication, and leadership.

Moving on. Departure is a difficult time for many advisers and postdocs. No adviser wants to lose a productive, well-qualified lab member. Nonetheless, advisers must remember that their goal as mentors is to help their postdocs to advance. Transitions may be eased if terms are specified by contract. Within these terms, the adviser can help to judge when the apprentice is ready to move to the next step.

The 'Special Something' that Brings Success

When Adam came to a federal laboratory as a postdoc in anthropology, he was intimidated by the competition in his field of Central American studies. His adviser, however, suggested he stop and think for a moment. He asked, What do you want to get out of this postdoctoral experience? What are your career goals? What special skills do you have that most other researchers in the field do not? What are some of the unique aspects of this research environment? Which of my connections or talents can help you?

In Adam's case, he spent part of his boyhood in Mexico. This provided him with unique language skills, contacts, and general understanding that most of his competition did not have. In addition, his university hosted a center of Latin American studies where he could increase his contacts with scholars interested in the same area.

Comment: *By working together, Adam and his adviser were able to develop a strategy that used the best of his assets—and provided him with an edge that could lift him a step above his competition.*

Best Practices

Even after a postdoc leaves, the adviser's role is not finished. Scientists and engineers change positions often, and advisers can be invaluable allies in helping with the next step along the career path, whenever it comes.

SUMMARY POINTS

➤ At the outset, advisers need to make clear their expectations of the postdoc and learn about the postdoc's own expectations.

➤ In return for the postdoc's contributions, the adviser should both provide scientific and technical training and help the postdoc acquire other necessary "career" skills, such as those that contribute to effective communication, publication, grant writing, and management.

➤ Frequent communication between postdoc and adviser helps prevent problems from growing into grievances.

➤ Attending professional meetings is one of the most important ways a postdoc can enhance professional visibility, gain confidence, and build a network of contacts.

➤ Postdocs need regular feedback on the quality and direction of their work, including written evaluations at least annually.

➤ The adviser should take the lead early and often in discussing ethical standards, including issues of authorship, credit, conflicts of interest, and other ethical dilemmas.

5

The Postdoc and the Institution

Institutions benefit in many ways from the presence and activities of post-docs. Most importantly, their work supports the overall intellectual strength of the institution. Successful postdocs help plan and carry out the institution's research programs, build alliances and intellectual bridges to other institutions, raise the reputation of laboratories and departments, mentor graduate students, and increase the inflow of grant support.

In return, institutions have the responsibility to support their postdocs with adequate compensation and benefits, a supportive infrastructure and working conditions, appropriate institutional recognition and standing, and mechanisms for advancing their careers and finding subsequent positions.

THE INSTITUTIONAL STATUS OF THE POSTDOC

In many government and industrial settings, postdocs are treated much like other researchers with regard to institutional status, compensation, and other benefits. In universities, however, most postdocs are identified and recruited by individual faculty members to work on specific research grants. The university's administration may have only an approximate picture of the postdoctoral population and provide few mechanisms to standardize benefits or institutional status. Postdocs may be regarded as benefiting a particular investigator rather than the institution as a whole. In such cases it is the postdoc who suffers, receiving uncertain or no institutional standing and inadequate levels of compensation and benefits.

Sample Surveys of Postdoctoral Populations

Some postdocs seeking to enhance their experience have started with basic questions: How many of us are there and how can we reach each other? This was the motivation at Baylor College of Medicine in 1997: "No faculty or administrator knew how many postdocs were working at Baylor," recalls an official, "let alone how to contact them." It took six months to design a survey that asked the right questions and to establish a web site. The survey asked for issues of importance to postdocs, how postdocs rated their tenure so far, and what goals and priorities should be set for the newly formed postdoc association.

Postdocs at the University of California at San Francisco conducted an extensive survey in 1996 that received 419 responses from 1,076 postdoctoral scholars (one-third with MDs, two-thirds with PhDs). Respondents, whose mean age was 32 years and half of whom were foreign, reported poor perceptions of the job market and of prospects for their own careers. These perceptions were most pessimistic when interactions with their mentors were infrequent. Of the PhD postdocs, 21 percent said they had prolonged their postdoctoral position because of difficulty in finding other employment. This finding led to a recommendation for improved career guidance, mentoring, and performance evaluations, and to ongoing efforts with the administration to enhance those functions.

The postdoctoral association at Johns Hopkins, founded by postdocs, gathers survey information annually from both program directors and postdocs. Of the program directors, it asks if their division: 1) has a committee to help with postdoctoral issues; 2) has a mentoring committee to provide guidance and evaluation of postdocs; 3) does annual performance reviews of postdocs; 4) has a formal orientation for new postdocs; and 5) pays for fellows' health benefits.

The exit survey of postdocs at Johns Hopkins has grown more sophisticated and extensive over the years, and now poses 81 questions on issues related to compensation, source of support, benefits, goals, responsibilities, career planning, mentoring, accomplishments, future employment, issues of concern, and family issues. The primary concerns of postdocs have changed somewhat over the years moving from personal to professional issues. In 1992, the greatest concerns were personal safety and health insurance; in 1997, the greatest concerns were salary levels and future job placement (Figure 5-1).

Best Practices

In its 1998 study of the postdoctoral experience, the AAU committee wrote that "...the lack of institutional oversight of postdoctoral appointments, coupled with the evolution of postdoctoral education in a number of disciplines into a virtual requirement for a tenure-track faculty appointment, creates an unacceptable degree of variability and instability in this aspect of the academic enterprise."[1] Through its meetings with postdocs and advisers, COSEPUP has found that uncertain status, low pay and benefits, and lack of professional recognition

---

[1]AAU, 1998. Cited above.

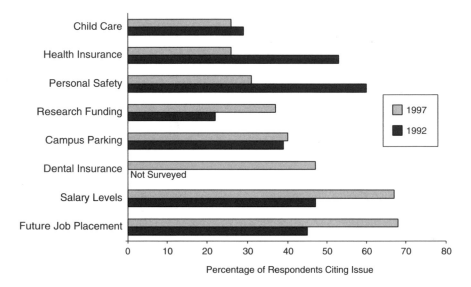

FIGURE 5-1: Primary Concerns of Postdoctorates at Johns Hopkins University. Source: Data collected by Johns Hopkins University Postdoctoral Association as presented in *Science,* 1999, Vol. 285, p. 1514.

are indeed issues of concern at many universities. This section describes those issues and lists initiatives that some institutions have found helpful.

Variations in titles. COSEPUP found that postdocs at universities expressed more frustration about their institutional status than those at national or industrial labs. Many of today's postdocs find themselves with a clear function but variable titles. Postdocs may be categorized as research associates, research assistant professors, contract employees, adjunct professors, laboratory instructors, research fellows, and so on, according to local custom (see Box). Such variations

---

How Are Postdocs Classified at Your Organizations?

Most of the organizations surveyed (50 percent) used the term "fellow" with smaller numbers classifying their postdocs as "employee" (40 percent), "trainee" (35 percent), "associate" (23 percent), "faculty" (13 percent), "student" (13 percent), and "staff" (10 percent).

The "other" ways to classify postdocs included "employees-in-training," "scholars," "visiting postdoctoral scholars," and "students in training."

COSEPUP Survey Results

have permitted significant differences in salary, taxation, health benefits, enrollment in a pension plan, periods of appointment, rehiring options, employment security, personal leave, and other aspects of professional life among people with the same work.

Recently, for example, one medical school counted 17 appointment categories for postdocs. After establishing a postdoctoral office, this number was reduced to three, and a uniform policy was applied to all. Other institutions report various systemic inequities. For example, postdoctoral researchers paid from the grants of advisers are usually considered temporary employees and qualify for employee health plans, parking facilities, vacations, and other benefits. Postdoctoral fellows, however, who have received their own funding directly, may be considered neither students nor employees and thus may or may not receive health benefits from (or through) their institution or lab. A standardized system of nomenclature can help avoid these inequities. (In addition, funding agencies, especially federal agencies, should require and fund health care benefits; see Chapter 6.) See Table 5-1 for a summary of some of the differences between classifying postdocs as a student or employee.

Another advantage of consistent status is that it can allow universities to track their postdoc populations after they finish their terms. This is extremely difficult when postdocs are paid and classified in widely different ways.

TABLE 5-1: Examples of Differences in Entitlements based on Classification of Postdocs as Students or Employees

If a postdoc were an **employee**, they might receive	If a postdoc were clearly a **student**, they might be entitled to . . . . .

• Fringe benefits, such as
  • Health insurance
  • Maternity leave
  • Retirement plan
• Employee grievance procedure
• Hours/wages protection
• Due process before termination
• Follow equal pay for equal work guidelines so that men and women are paid equivalently
• Access employee assistance and other services provided to employees
• Serve as a principal investigator
• Foreign post-docs would need H1 visas
	• Use the student health center and mental health center
	• Use student recreational facilities and entertainment discounts (e.g., to athletic events, plays, etc.)
	• Access student housing
	• Receive exemption from some taxes, such as FICA
	• Use student placement facilities
	• Access student grievance procedure
	• Register for courses
	• Foreign post-docs would need J visas.

Note: These are two extremes. There are categories of employees who fall in between these two categories.

INCORPORATING THE POSTDOC INTO THE INSTITUTION

Institutions have taken a variety of steps to incorporate postdocs into their programs and classifications structure. This section examines postdoctoral policies, offices, and other mechanisms that respond to the needs of postdocs.

Establishing institutional policies. The first step in improving the status of postdocs is to establish institutional policies for them. This often begins with a simplified classification scheme. At the University of Notre Dame, the Graduate Council's Postdoc Committee recommended a new category of employee for "postdoctoral scholars," distinct from students, faculty, or staff and placed under the supervision of the graduate school. Each institution needs to adopt policy guidelines that both suit its particular mission and gain the support of postdocs and faculty.

Because of their hybrid training-and-working status, postdocs do not easily fit into simple categories at most institutions. Many institutions have struggled with this challenge, with different results: At Vanderbilt University the postdoc is a research fellow; at the University of Iowa, a postdoctoral scholar; at Stanford University, a student; at Eli Lilly, a postdoctoral scientist/fixed-duration employee.

The vast University of California system tackled this issue in 1998. The Council of Graduate Deans' Report on Postdoctoral Education recommended that "Postdoctoral scholars should be constituted as a distinct group of individuals ... clearly separate from students, other academic employees, staff employees, and resident and house staff..." Although they did not indicate their reason for this decision, it was presumably because the nature of research funding determined the classification of postdocs. The council recommended at least two sets of appointment titles: One set, for postdocs who are paid by an adviser's research grants, must be employees and "therefore require academic titles," another set, for postdocs funded through fellowships and traineeships, are not considered employees. The San Diego campus decided on three titles: postdoctoral fellow (individual awarded a fellowship), postdoctoral trainee (supported by a UCSD training grant), and postdoctoral scholar (neither a fellow nor a trainee).[2]

The Mayo Graduate School of the Mayo Clinic, which considers itself a "hybrid academic/industrial environment," devised a different solution. Postdocs are considered "valued professionals in their final stages of development" and are offered a clear progression of positions from training toward full employment. The progression includes research fellow (up to three years), senior research fellow (3-7 years), research associate (a springboard to independence), senior research technologist (employment in technology), and professional associate in research (employment in research). Mayo believes that "some mix of temporary and permanent research workers is necessary to achieve the end results."

---

[2]See web site saawww.ucsf.edu/psa/

An adviser at the University of Pittsburgh concludes: "Nobody's categories are perfect. Each institution has to devise something that works. The postdocs should get the best of both worlds, not the worst of both worlds."

Establishing a postdoctoral office. A second helpful step in improving the status of postdocs is to assign an officer the job of monitoring postdoctoral policies and providing advice and resources. At present, it is common for postdocs in universities to lack a "point person" who can answer their questions and provide information. At the University of Colorado, all postdocs are now appointed through a central office, which allows that institution to apply appropriate policies and track its postdoc population.

One goal of postdoc offices is to ensure consistent application of policies. The University of California at San Francisco, for example, now requires a formal hiring letter, jointly signed by the faculty mentor and department chair or other university official, along with a statement of goals, policies, and responsibilities applicable to postdoctoral education. These details include expected duration of support, compensation, and benefits. Initial postdoctoral appointments may last no longer than two to three years, and can be extended only when adviser and postdoc jointly agree that renewal would advance the postdoc's career. As a general rule, total time spent is limited to six years.

A postdoctoral office can accomplish other useful functions: organize orientation and professional development programs; maintain a career center; publish an orientation manual; encourage best practices by mentors; act as a liaison between postdocs, advisers, and administrators; provide a certificate of completion; and keep a directory of the postdoctoral population, including more experienced postdocs who are willing to mentor new arrivals. Some offices help postdocs learn about research program development, job seeking, grant writing, teaching, the mechanics of running a lab, and other professional skills, such as management, negotiation, meeting organization, and conflict resolution.

A well-conceived postdoctoral office is sensitive to the needs of the adviser as well as to those of the postdoc. "It would seem that a postdoctoral office is logical if it helps define the postdoc's status," said one adviser. "But if it restrains the way the PI can do science, it won't work."

The structure of a postdoctoral office will vary with the institution and size of the postdoctoral population. An existing office for graduate students can handle many functions for postdocs as well. Some of the needs of foreign postdocs may be met by an existing office of international students.

In terms of staffing, two kinds of expertise are useful. The first is a person with postdoctoral and research experience who can offer informed advice to both faculty and postdocs. The second is a human resources person with expertise in student, staff, and faculty issues.

The expense of a postdoctoral office is borne by the institution; however, costs are usually low because many functions are already staffed for other popu-

Creating a Postdoctoral Office

At the *University of Pennsylvania*, some 680 of the 1,000 postdocs work at the medical school. The Office of Postdoctoral Programs drew on a year-long series of interviews between medical school officials and postdocs to create a coherent plan which was able to:

- Offer dual leadership for the office: a faculty researcher who can discuss laboratory and mentoring issues, and two persons trained in human resource issues;
- Design a template for an appointment letter and compile an orientation package containing information on health insurance, housing, visas, taxes, off-campus living, the registration process, and other postdoc issues; faculty use both the letter and package to inform appointees;
- Standardize postdoc appointment procedure and employment policies, including stipends based on the *NIH National Research Service Award (NRSA)* scale, a six-week parental leave policy, and uniform health benefits;
- Initiate a database of information on postdocs, including date and institution of terminal degree, discipline, research specialty, publications, and visa status (45 percent of the postdocs at Penn are foreign postdocs).

From the outset, planners realized that the office needed to serve not only the postdocs but also their faculty advisers. They created a web page that PIs can use to list their postdoc openings. The web page is advertised in *Science* and *Nature*, at no cost to the PI, and has links to postdoctoral associations and other resources. A postdoctoral association was formed to represent the postdocs.

Another pioneering postdoctoral office was started at *Albert Einstein College of Medicine* four years ago. In addition to many of the functions at Penn, Einstein also sends a letter to all advisers after a postdoc has been in their lab for 18-24 months, advising them that it may be time for a salary increase. In the fourth year a more extensive letter asks for each postdoc's CV and publication record. The adviser and department chair are then asked to decide whether the postdoc will be renewed for a fifth year, and what might be expected after that; additional years require faculty-level benefits. This policy effectively places a cap on postdoctoral terms.

The *University of Alabama at Birmingham* established an Office of Postdoctoral Education for its 325 postdocs in 1999. It serves as "a natural extension of the existing services already being offered to graduate students, and emphasizes the training aspects and formal communication link" between postdocs and the administration. The explicit goal of the office is to provide opportunities for postdocs to identify and acquire skills needed for successful career development. A second goal is to "enhance the postdoctoral experience by promoting intellectual growth and facilitating the goals of mentors and scholars." The office provides a model acceptance letter, specifies an appointment procedure (and provides a checklist), conducts a mandatory orientation for new appointees, sets a term of four years (with the possibility of extension to five), and maintains a "postdoctoral scholar applicant tracking system."

Best Practices

lations at the institution. A few institutions levy a small per capita fee on departments that hire postdocs.

An institution cannot always solve practical problems of housing, parking, and day care, especially in large and/or expensive cities. But even basic informational resources can improve morale and speed the search for a dwelling or other resource. As one dean put it, "Every minute a postdoc spends looking for a parking space is a minute lost from more productive activities."

Career guidance. A primary function of the postdoctoral office is to provide support for postdocs who are searching for jobs. While advisers are often best positioned to contact and suggest potential employers in their own field, a postdoctoral office can offer job counseling for other fields or sectors, coordinate and publicize recruiter visits, maintain contacts with former postdocs, post job openings, and hold workshops on employment trends. A career office can also assist with the basic mechanics of job seeking: how to write a CV, prepare a cover letter, organize slides for a talk, and so on. Especially helpful are statistics on recent jobs taken by postdocs, especially permanent positions. According to COSEPUP's survey, only a few institutions have career service offices that are focused on postdocs (see Box).

A central postdoctoral office constitutes not only a practical resource but also a focal point to unite a dispersed population that may number a thousand or more. At the same time, each large division or school (e.g., the school of engineering, arts and sciences, etc.) needs to address its own particular postdoc population. For example, the Department of Medicine at Johns Hopkins designates a faculty member to discuss professional or personal issues related to the post doctoral experience with any postdoc or faculty member.

Postdocs need the most assistance when they first arrive. Argonne National Laboratory provides a Newcomers' Office, whose offerings range from lists of recent appointments (to introduce newcomers) to recycled furniture for arriving families. A volunteer spouse's program is also available.

Does Your Organization Provide Job Placement Services for Your Postdocs?

About half do . . . either as part of general student/employee services, through the adviser, or from an assigned individual whose sole responsibility is to work with postdocs (and/or graduate students). For the other half, job placement is the dual responsibility of the adviser and the postdoc. A few organizations mentioned such resources as career centers, job fairs, job placement web sites, and general student services. Several reported that job placement activities are localized and vary by institutional unit.

COSEPUP Survey Results

Developing 'Survival Skills'

In addition to their disciplinary training, postdocs need additional career or "survival" skills to maximize their chances for a rewarding career. A Postdoctoral Taskforce at the *University of Pittsburgh* has developed a detailed program to educate postdocs on such topics as:

- How to choose a postdoctoral adviser
- What should and should not be expected from an adviser
- How to establish goals for a postdoctoral experience
- Intellectual property rights
- The resources available at their institution
- How to build a community of mentors
- How to develop a professional network
- How and when to become independent
- How to leave the institution on good terms

As a key mechanism, the task force has developed a Survival Skills and Ethics Workshop for postdocs, graduate students, and faculty. The workshop, held several times a year, offers programs and advice on such topics as writing research articles, making oral presentations, job hunting, teaching, writing grant proposals, personnel and project management, and responsible conduct.

Similarly, the *NIH* fellows organization sponsors three skills development seminars a year for its on-campus fellows. Topics include writing, speaking, and teaching; it has also arranged for a fall job fair, extra travel awards, and adjunct jobs teaching in the evenings.

Postdocs often need help with practical questions: How do the requirements of research institutions differ from those of undergraduate teaching colleges? What kinds of internships provide the best preparation for professional careers? How is an industry job search different from a university job search? What different skills are required?

Best Practices

Benefits. Some of the most gifted postdocs come with fellowships, both from US and foreign sources, and yet they are often disadvantaged in terms of employment benefits. The institution has the responsibility either to provide equitable health insurance and other benefits or to require individual laboratories or departments to provide them. In addition, the institution should notify postdocs about the availability of benefits. According to COSEPUP's survey of institutions, many postdocs are either not notified about their benefits status or are ineligible for standard institutional benefits. The majority of institutions in the survey did not offer dental insurance, retirement plans, parental leave, personal

---

Postdoc Handbooks

One of the early priorities of most postdoctoral associations (or postdoctoral offices) is to produce a handbook to orient postdocs to institutional and area services. The *NIH Fellows' Handbook*, produced by the Fellows' Committee, could be considered the granddaddy of postdoc handbooks, offering nearly 60 categories of information from Acronyms Used at the NIH to Washington Metropolitan Area Activities. There are informative sections on appointments, conflict resolution, ethical conduct, housing, leave policy, mentoring, ombudsperson services, parking, postfellowship employment, research conduct, and many other topics.

The fundamental goals of the Fellows' Committee, as explained in the Handbook, include promoting education and career development, fostering communication among fellows and within the larger NIH community, helping inform fellows about policies, and serving as a liaison to the administration.

Similarly, the *NRC's Research Associateship program* produces the *Policies, Practices, and Procedures: A Handbook for Research Associateship Awardees* to serve its approximately 700 associates, most of whom work in national laboratories. The handbook has chapters on definitions, accepting an award and beginning tenure, stipends, visas, insurance, taxes, travel, relocating, patents and publications, renewing an award, and terminating an award. Like most handbooks, this one is found on the web.[3]

---

[3]For NIH, see ftp://helix.nih.gov/felcom/index.html; for NRC, http://www.nas.edu/rap

---

Best Practices

---

leave, cost-of-living salary adjustments, day care, life insurance, sick leave, or disability insurance. (See Box.)

Most nonacademic organizations offered both orientation sessions to discuss benefits and information about benefits with the letter of acceptance.

OTHER RESPONSIBILITIES OF THE INSTITUTION

There are many useful steps the institution can take, not only by offering services but also by publicizing best practices that help integrate postdocs into the institution and make their work more productive.

Mentoring. Mentoring is the specific responsibility of the adviser. Institutions can help promote better mentoring practices that enhance the postdoctoral experience and reduce the chance of neglect or abuse. Simple mechanisms like mentoring awards can raise public awareness of the need for guidance. Even the signature of a division head or chair on the postdoc's admission document symbolically raises the institution's responsibility for the postdoc. The institution

Which of the Following Benefits Is Provided at Full Compensation to All Postdocs, Regardless of Adviser or Funding Source?

At academic organizations, the only benefits offered by more than half the respondents were e-mail accounts, library access, and vacation time. Smaller numbers offered on-campus parking or the equivalent (45 percent), sick leave (45 percent), parental leave (31 percent), dental insurance (28 percent), and disability insurance (28 percent). Only 7 percent offered child care, and 10 percent paid travel expenses to conferences where the postdoc would be presenting.

Benefits at nonacademic institutions were relatively generous. Nearly 90 percent offered dental insurance, disability insurance, e-mail accounts, vacation time, sick leave, and life insurance. More than half offered parental leave, parking, retirement funds, and library access. One-third offered child care and cost-of-living salary adjustments.

How Is the Postdoc Made Aware of Benefits that Are and Are Not Available?

From academic organizations, the three largest categories with similar numbers of responses were as follows: 1) the adviser bore the responsibility of discussing benefits with the postdoc, 2) an orientation meeting where benefits were discussed was offered to all entering postdocs, and 3) each postdoc received a letter before arrival that outlined the organization's policies. Three organizations explicitly stated that no information on benefits was formally provided, and additional comments indicated that some institutions report this information informally or have initiated a process of including benefits information in an acceptance letter.

COSEPUP Survey Results

can also include mentoring in its guidelines for faculty review and offer to provide training for advisers in effective communication and evaluation techniques.[4] Finally, institutions can encourage postdocs to acquire teaching and other professional skills by recognizing the development of those skills as a worthwhile use of research funds. (See also box on mentoring in previous chapter.)

Mentoring committees. Some institutions are experimenting with the use of formal and informal mentoring committees, selected by the postdoc, that meet every six or twelve months. The purpose of such a committee is not to alter the primary role of the adviser, but to provide additional perspective and guidance, as well as help in building a professional network. A committee can also help to

---

[4]For further details and examples, see the National Academies' *Adviser, Teacher, Role Model, Friend: On Being a Mentor to Students in Science and Engineering,* 1997, available via the web (www.nap.edu/readingroom/books/mentor).

What Neutral Parties Are Responsible for Handling Grievances of the Postdoc?

Responses to this question indicated a wide diversity of mechanisms. The largest number of organizations (76 percent) said that a dean or department chair handled grievances; smaller numbers pointed to a human-resources staff person (51 percent), the adviser (46 percent), or an ombudsperson (43 percent). Institutions reported a wide variety of "other" methods for handling postdocs' grievances, from "same as junior faculty" to "office of grad studies and research" and "ombudsfolks—faculty peer adviser selected by postdocs"). A few reported that most of the responsibility lay with a single person; a smaller number described a more flexible process ("Dispute resolution guideline for College of Medicine postdoctoral fellows; Ad hoc committee makes recommendation to associate dean for research and graduate education").

COSEPUP Survey Results

---

counter the isolation experienced by many postdocs, especially those from overseas, and protect against the occasional instances of abuse.

It is true that experienced investigators have little time to spare for additional duties. However, postdocs have found that even brief discussions (one to two hours per meeting) can bring valuable rewards in new perspectives and suggestions.

Ethical development. Institutions should emphasize the importance of professional development and ethics as a central feature of mentoring. By establishing seminars or workshops on research conduct and ethics, the institution can supplement what is learned from the adviser and provide a baseline code of behavior for all postdocs.[5]

Grievances. The imbalance of power in the adviser-postdoc relationship increases the possibility of misunderstandings and abuses. A desire for a grievance procedure is commonly reported by postdoc surveys, and the AAU recommends that each institution's core policies should provide mechanisms to resolve grievances. The University of California system, for example, recommends that campuses establish a standard grievance procedure for postdocs that is written, protects due process, contains clear time lines, and requires a clear statement of alleged grievance and requested remedy.[6] The COSEPUP survey shows that institutions handle grievances through a variety of mechanisms (see Box).

---

[5]As referenced earlier, the National Academies' publication, O*n Being a Scientist: Responsible Conduct in Research,* 1995, may be useful in such discussions.

[6]Council on Graduate Deans, University of California, *Report on Postdoctoral Education at UC,* Fall 1998. See web site www.ogsr.ucsd.edu/PostdocEdu/Report.html.

The role of the ombudsperson. What can a postdoc do when he believes his department chair or other senior scientist should just be thanked in a paper's acknowledgements, but the adviser insists on including such individuals as co-authors? What can a postdoc do when she is told to work on a project in which she has no interest?

One reason grievances are difficult for postdocs to resolve is that they often arise from the decisions or actions of their advisers. Similarly, deans or department chairs may be seen as siding with the institution. In an attempt to provide an independent and impartial person to assist in resolving disputes or misunderstandings, some institutions have found that an ombudsperson can be helpful. An ombudsperson serves as an informal information resource, receives complaints, and assists in resolving disputes on a confidential basis. The ombudsperson is a facilitator, not a decision maker.

One university dean praised his institution's ombudsperson as a sympathetic and confidential person to whom postdocs can turn. The NIH, which has some 2,800 postdocs on its main campus, has hired an ombudsperson to head a Cooperative Resolution Center, defined as "a neutral site for resolving work-related conflicts."

Special needs of foreign nationals. Postdocs on temporary visas comprise approximately half of all postdocs in the US. Many need help, both before and after they arrive, in resolving visa questions, finding housing, meeting other postdocs, and arranging bank accounts, credit cards, driver's licenses, and Social Security numbers. Because of cultural and language barriers, foreign postdocs also experience far more social isolation than US postdocs, which potentially reduces their contributions as teachers, research collaborators, and members of the community. (For a thorough discussion of visas, see the US Department of State's web site at travel.state.gov/visa;exchange.html.)

Many institutions can respond to such needs simply by publicizing an already existing office of international affairs. Access to information about visa issues and grant requirements, in particular, can make an institution far more attractive to foreign scientists and engineers, and increase the possibility that the best of them will choose that institution. Stanford University has enhanced its visa processing by contracting with an outside specialist.[7]

Foreign postdocs often need encouragement in strengthening their command of English. Postdoc advisers at Vanderbilt University have found that verbal skills are the best indicators of overall career success, and that those with poor English require an average of two more years to find US jobs than those with language proficiency.

---

[7]Visa requests at Stanford's School of Medicine originate in the sponsoring department and are then routed through the Office of Postdoctoral Affairs for approval and forwarded to the Bechtel International Center for processing. Bechtel, which is able to process J-1 requests in one week, also offers seminars for administrators on visa completion.

Does the Organization Have Staff Who Deal Specifically with the Special Needs of Non-US or Foreign National Postdocs?

Most respondents (70 percent) answered yes; only 8 percent answered no, and 8 percent reported that the needs of non-US postdocs were handled by the adviser.

Most of the "other" responses indicated a pattern of offering postdocs the same access to international services as students and other scholars.

If Offered, in What Areas Do Foreign National Postdocs Receive Assistance?

Virtually all respondents (97 percent) assisted foreign nationals with visa issues, and more than half offered assistance with tax issues, housing, and English language studies. Smaller numbers reported assisting with Social Security questions (43 percent), driver's licenses (11 percent), and credit references (11 percent).

Several institutions offered help with household furnishings and support groups for spouses and dependents.

COSEPUP Survey Results

Postdoctoral associations. One of the postdoc's most common complaints is a feeling of isolation and the lack of a peer group through which to communicate with the institution. Postdoctoral associations can fill both needs, helping to build community and improve communication. Because postdocs are a transient population, these associations need institutional support to survive. An institution that encourages a postdoctoral association signals to postdoctoral candidates that their concerns are taken seriously.

These new associations (one of the first was founded at Johns Hopkins in 1992) sometimes begin with the indispensable step of counting the number of postdocs at an institution, as was the case at the University of California at San Francisco (see Box, *Postdoctoral Associations*). The UCSF Postdoctoral Scholars Association, formed in 1995, has worked with the university to formalize a grievance process, bring postdoc representatives to committees that set postdoctoral policy, establish an annual orientation for postdocs, and offer access to group health insurance.

Postdocs working in industry settings have also formed productive associations. At Eli Lilly & Co., for example, three postdoctoral fellows form the Postdoctoral Scientist Council, which "...serves to enhance the scientific and social experience of postdocs at Lilly." The council has organized a research forum for postdocs, arranged on-and off-site social gatherings, suggested seminar speakers to address issues of interest to postdocs (e.g., how industry recruits for senior

Is There a Postdoctoral Association or the Equivalent at Your Institution?

Most organizations (58 percent) reported that no postdoctoral associations are available. Just over one-fourth reported the presence of postdoctoral associations run by the postdocs themselves. In some cases, postdoc associations or councils are run by the institution.

The "other" responses included one other postdoctoral association run by postdocs and called a "postdoctoral council." One institution reported an association run jointly by postdocs and the institution. Most indicated that postdoctoral activities were either informal, located within a laboratory or department, or focused on a particular group (such as a group of Chinese students and scholars).

If Your Organization Has a Postdoctoral Association or Equivalent, What Are Its Main Functions?

Almost all these organizations (93 percent) reported that postdoctoral associations provided professional and social activities for postdocs. Most (79 percent) said that the associations acted as liaison between postdocs and administration. Half noted that associations provided information for postdocs on issues of general interest, and some (36 percent) said that the associations appointed representatives to the organizations' administrative councils.

COSEPUP Survey Results

positions, how to make the transition from postdoc to senior scientist), and proposed improvements to the postdoc program (e.g., a seminar/round table series, an orientation package for incoming postdocs, additional training in communication, leadership, and mentoring).

COSEPUP's survey indicated that only a small minority of institutions have formed postdoctoral associations. The primary goals of existing associations are to provide a liaison with the administration and to provide professional and social activities for postdocs (see Box).

Stabilizing the postdoctoral population. Institutions, notably universities, have a role to play in monitoring the number of postdocs (and graduate students) admitted to their programs, especially in the high-growth areas of the life sciences. As the NRC *Trends* report stated, investigators and training-program directors accept large numbers of students in part to meet their faculties' need for instructors and laboratory workers.[8] That committee urged life-science faculties

---

[8]Office of Scientific and Engineering Personnel, National Research Council, *Trends in the Early Careers of Life Scientists,* Washington, DC: National Academy Press, 1998.

Postdoctoral Associations

The first postdoctoral association, organized at *Johns Hopkins School of Medicine* in 1992, grew out of a concern for safety when several postdocs were assaulted outside the laboratory at night.

"Before we started," recalls current co-president Lisa Koslowski, "we had no benefits, no salary guidelines, and morale was very low. Now we have minimum salary guidelines on the NIH model, health benefits, and a good relationship with the institution. When we bring issues to them, such as safe parking facilities, they are more than willing to help us. In the last few months we've worked out a plan for dental insurance." To stay abreast of current concerns, the group conducts annual surveys of all postdocs, including entrance and exit interviews.

Postdocs at the *University of California at San Francisco* formed their Postdoctoral Scholars Association (PSA) from a variety of motivations: to create a resource and sense of identity for a largely undefined group, out of the "frustration that PhD scientists feel when they compare their career and mentoring with those of medical professionals," and out of concern about career prospects for biomedical scientists. The PSA later combined with the Graduate Students Association to spur the creation of a Career Office for Scientists, which offers career counseling, helps with the mechanics of résumé preparation and effective interviewing, and compiles databases of alumni who have connections in academia and industry.

Postdocs at the *National Institute of Environmental Health Sciences* in North Carolina's Research Triangle Park developed a Trainees' Assembly "to foster the professional advancement of postdocs, visiting, and predoctoral fellows and other non-tenured, non-permanent scientists." The group disseminates information at a web site, publishes an *Orientation Handbook*, and sponsors a seminar series where trainees can present research projects or lectures and receive critiques. They also have forums on professional topics (e.g., grant writing, industrial and non-academic positions), a science fair with local scientific colleagues, a distinguished lecturer lunch, outreach activities in the community, and monthly pizza socials.

A group at *Albert Einstein College of Medicine* was formed in 1996, according to cofounder Paula Cohen, to revitalize its postdoctoral programs and image. "Einstein was faced with the problem of being the poor cousin of New York institutions." Dominant themes in the response to a survey of postdocs were insufficient mentoring, a lack of interaction with other labs, and limited teaching opportunities. Most of the group's suggestions for improvements had to do with increased information and interpersonal contact. The administration was supportive in designing a series of reforms to improve career guidance, mentoring, and the overall quality of postdoc life.

Best Practices

to seek alternatives to these workforce needs by increasing the number of permanent laboratory workers, and to consider restricting the numbers of graduate students supported on research grants.

Although this COSEPUP report does not specify mechanisms for stabilizing the postdoctoral population, it does reiterate the concerns of the *Trends* report with respect both to hiring more permanent laboratory workers and restraining the size of the postdoctoral population. Mechanisms should be adopted by individual institutions. For example, an institution might restrict the employment of postdocs whose stipends/salaries fall below a certain level. If adequate compensation is not provided by the funding organization, the institution would then appoint the postdoc only if supplementary funding is made available.

Some early predictions that postdoctoral associations would become adversarial or union-like organizations have not materialized. Leaders of the Johns Hopkins association, for example, describe their group as a vehicle for sharing information with one another and communicating their concerns to the administration. "There is no need for a union," said one member, "when communication is open."

Informing graduate students about the postdoctoral experience. Many, and perhaps most, postdocs begin their appointment without a clear idea of what to expect from the experience. The success of an appointment may depend heavily on early communication with the adviser about expectations and responsibilities. Therefore, institutions and mentors of graduate students have an important role to play in educating them about the postdoctoral experience before they decide to undertake this advanced training. Important questions to consider are the level of their own research skills, training needs, and career goals. For further discussion of career decision making, see COSEPUP's "Careers" guide, cited in the bibliography.

SUMMARY POINTS

➤ In many institutions, the administration may have only an approximate picture of the postdoctoral population and no policy to standardize institutional status or benefits.

➤ An important step is to establish postdoctoral policies on such matters as titles, expected terms, and institutional status. This status may strongly affect benefits and other financial issues.

➤ Some institutions have established a postdoctoral office or officer to serve as an information resource for postdocs and to organize programs for postdoc orientation, professional development, and career services. Such an office can also encourage good mentoring, act as liaison between postdocs, advisers, and administrators, and track the postdoctoral population.

➤ Many institutions offer financial and logistical support for postdoctoral associations, which constitute a vehicle for discussing issues of concern to postdocs, building a social network, and communicating with the administration.

➤ Some institutions are experimenting with the use of "mentoring committees" to provide additional perspective and guidance to the postdoc.

➤ Institutions can help resolve grievances by establishing mechanisms, including an ombudsperson, to work toward conflict resolution.

➤ Each institution should ensure that foreign postdocs have a resource person or office to advise them on such issues as acculturation, visa compliance, income taxes, and language skills.

6

The Postdoc and the Funding Organization

The quality of the postdoctoral experience is influenced in important ways by granting agencies and mechanisms of financial support for scientific and engineering research. By tradition, research in the US has dual objectives: 1) the discovery and application of new knowledge, and 2) the education of the scientists and engineers who perform research. Funding organizations can help ensure that the second goal is not neglected with regard to postdocs.

The educational aspect of research is highly visible in the university, and it should also characterize federal and industrial laboratories where scientists-in-training learn in the company of experienced researchers. Funding organizations can play an important role in promoting the educational component of research by encouraging career development and guidance, as well as more focused scientific and technical training.

LEVELS OF FUNDING

A source of dissatisfaction among many postdocs, especially those in the life sciences who work at universities, is the relatively low pay. The federal agencies that support research, especially the NIH and NSF, have a dominant position in establishing compensation levels. In the life sciences, the NIH supports about 7,000 postdocs via NRSA traineeships, about 6,500 through research grants, and 2,800 through fellowships for trainees at its main campus in Bethesda, Maryland. Even after a recent increase of 25 percent in the NRSA stipend level, the starting level is only $26,256 per year. Although the NIH did not intend that this level serve as a national benchmark for setting postdoc salaries, it is widely interpreted as such by PIs who pay postdocs from their research grants. They or the institution may or may not supplement the "NIH scale" to raise the pay levels of postdocs.

The NIH defines awards to NRSA recipients not as salaries but as stipends for those who are receiving training. In this sense, a stipend is intended as a mechanism for sharing costs among the funder, the host institution, and the trainee (in the form of research performed and income foregone). The mechanism's underlying assumption is that the trainee receive, in addition to the stipend, both scientific instruction and career guidance that can lead to improved abilities and career satisfaction.

The postdoctoral experience succeeds when this assumption is shared by all parties and when oversight and guidance are adequate. The experience does not succeed when the educational component is weak and when the stipend becomes, by default, the only compensation for a postdoc's contributions to the program.

The NIH, NSF, and other funding organizations do not use a particular benchmark to establish stipend levels. According to NIH officials, the recent increase in stipends resulted from a substantial rise in agency funding and a general feeling that stipends were too low (before October 1998, postdoc stipends began at $19,000 annually).

COSEPUP concluded during its investigation that present compensation levels are probably still too low for the optimal functioning of the research enterprise. Although stipends should not be the primary incentive for accepting a postdoc appointment, neither should they be a large disincentive; without adequate pay, it is reasonable to conclude that fewer of America's best students will elect to pursue careers in research.

One way to quantify reasonable stipend levels is through a "functional" strategy. That is, the total cost to the institution or professor of hiring a postdoc should not be less than that of hiring a research assistant or technician with the same number of years of experience subsequent to their last degree. At present, it is commonly the case that postdocs are paid appreciably less than technicians with a recent bachelor's or master's degree. Even though a postdoc's compensation should include career development, the primary grievance of many postdocs is that they are treated as "cheap labor," even after five or more years of post-bachelor's experience.

SOURCES OF FUNDING

The funding source defines not only the stipend level and other financial features of the grant, but also the degree of accountability of the grantee. When postdocs are supported on the research grants of PIs, they are essentially hired to work on particular projects in specific locations. The organizations that provide this grant money (such as federal agencies) award grant money to the institution where the investigator works. Some of this money provides salaries for people designated by the investigator, who may be postdocs, graduate students, technicians, or others.

Such grants to PIs provide the resources for much of the nation's academic research. From the PI's point of view, the grants afford a necessary degree of continuity for research projects and the availability of postdocs provides them with the ability to hire talented researchers at relatively low salaries. From the point of view of the funding organization, the grants enable the performance of research to meet national objectives. At the same time, it is difficult for funding organizations to influence the experience of postdocs (or graduate students) so as to ensure educational activities and opportunities for career advancement. Unless postdocs are identifiable in grant reports as postdocs (often they are not), it is also difficult to monitor their activities or subsequent careers.

The second common category of funding awards includes competitive, "portable" fellowships that postdocs may take to any institution or laboratory where they are accepted. Such fellowships, which support a small minority (perhaps 15 percent) of the postdoctoral population, are offered by a wide variety of organizations, including the NSF, NIH, private foundations, and foreign governments. Organizations that award fellowships can and should track their recipients more closely and influence the quality of the experience more directly. One way they can influence the experience is to inform recipients about best practices and hold advisers accountable for a certain level of mentoring and evaluation.

The most common fellowships are the NIH NRSAs. About 5,500 NRSAs (the F-32) are awarded directly to postdocs in the biomedical, behavioral, and clinical areas with the stipulation that they must identify in their application a sponsoring institution and adviser. One advantage of F-32s is that recipients can use them at any institution willing to serve as sponsor (including NIH or other government facilities). About 1,500 NRSAs in a different category (T-35) are awarded directly to institutions to support the training of postdocs in basic or clinical aspects of health science.

From the postdocs' point of view, transportable funding may provide greater flexibility to gain teaching experience, pursue coursework, shift specialties, or rotate to other labs or sectors. In some national laboratories, such as the National Institute of Standards and Technology (NIST), transportable funding makes it possible, for example, for postdocs to change advisers if the relationship is not mutually productive.

OPPORTUNITIES OF FUNDING ORGANIZATIONS

One way funding organizations can enhance the postdoctoral experience is to tie the grant approval process more closely to good mentoring practices.

Broader impacts. As models, some federal grants request that applicants for research grants provide evidence of mentoring ability. The NSF requires researchers who have received prior investigator grants to describe, when requesting additional funding, "any contribution to the development of human resources in science and engineering." The NSF has also begun to ask (in 1997) for information about the "broader impacts" of a proposed research program, including anticipated effects on social, educational, and racial conditions.

In addition to asking the adviser about plans for training the postdoc, the NIH's NRSA application form asks for information about the sponsor's previous trainees, including the total number of trainees, and requests more detailed information about a "representative five," including present employer and position. Funding agencies should extend this practice to request written evidence of the history of an adviser's research and mentoring experience (e.g., publications where their former postdocs were lead authors, subsequent employment, etc.) so they can evaluate the potential advisers suitability for supervising a postdoc.

Promoting best practices. Funding organizations can take other steps to improve the postdoctoral experience. All postdocs can benefit from attending professional meetings, yet many lack sufficient funds to do so. Funding organizations can provide competitive travel grants for this purpose. They can also provide grants (such as the Burroughs Wellcome transitional awards) to senior postdocs (sometimes promoted by universities to non-tenure track faculty positions such as research assistant professor) to help in the transition to full-time positions. The period after a postdoc can bring great uncertainty and additional time may be needed to write grant proposals and/or seek the next research position.

Funding organizations can specifically encourage certain activities by postdocs, such as authoring papers, mentoring technicians and graduate students, and especially teaching. By including such best practices in the language of research grants, funders can open the way for adoption by institutions and advisers.

Funding can be designed to promote collaborations and reduce the isolation of postdocs. One new model is the NSF's grants for Vertical Integration of Research and Education in the Mathematical Sciences (VIGRE). The VIGRE program was designed to support innovative educational and career-enhancing programs involving the collective participation of undergraduates, graduate students, postdoctoral fellows, and faculty.

Funding temporary employment. Funding organizations can also begin to adjust to new realities of the research environment, where temporary employment is now common. When postdocs who have completed their terms find themselves in such positions, they should be considered professional researchers and compensated as such—even if they have not achieved a tenured or other long-term position. Funding organizations can allocate a portion of their funding to interim positions for nontenured or temporary research scientists, in recognition of the altered progression of science careers.

The 'perennial postdoc.' Funding mechanisms can help to address the phenomenon of the "perennial postdoc." For example, organizations can design their grants in ways that differentiate between 1) PhDs who are in years 1-5 of their postdoctoral research (primarily a training phase) and 2) PhDs who are in semi-permanent or permanent status as research scientists. Postdocs in the second category would not be considered to be "in training"; instead, they would be considered employees, with commensurate standing, pay, and benefits.

Addressing some inequities of funding. Funding organizations can also help eliminate inequities from the postdoctoral experience. For example, a postdoc who begins work on the adviser's grant might win a more prestigious fellowship. At some institutions, however, the postdoc could then lose health and other benefits which may not be ensured under the new fellowship. Funding organizations can work toward equitable provision of benefits across all granting mechanisms. The Howard Hughes Medical Institute, for example, stipulates that $5,000 of its institutional allowance for each postdoc must go into benefits.

Other inequities may arise when postdocs receive small grants from nongovernmental organizations, foreign governments, or other entities. Such entities should recognize that host institutions might not supplement low stipends/salaries, even though they are inadequate to live on. These funding organizations should consider requiring supplemental funding as a condition of awarding such a fellowship and/or reducing the number of postdocs funded in order to raise the stipend/salary to an appropriate level.

Communicating with funding organizations. For the largest funding organizations, notably the NIH and NSF, postdocs have no mechanism for communicating directly or regularly with the organization about the funding process or other issues of concern. Lack of communication may be especially important for postdocs supported on research grants, which are channeled through an institution. A communication mechanism would create a much-needed means for postdocs to obtain information directly from the funding organization and to communicate it to their postdoctoral association or institution. A national network of these associations, already connected via e-mail, is currently being formed, which would further expedite communication.

Promoting good mentoring. There are many ways in which funders can design their proposal forms so as to promote good mentoring. By publicizing the goal of human resource development as vigorously as the goal of research, they would raise the value of mentoring and career guidance. Funding organizations can request evaluations that describe activities such as the use of mentoring committees for postdocs, efforts to limit the length of appointments, encouragement of teaching and mentoring by postdocs, and other steps that can advance the careers of postdocs.

The NIH's Mentored Research Scientist Development Award (K01) directly promotes good mentoring. Specifically, it "provides an intensive, supervised career development experience" for a junior research scientist supervised by a more experienced investigator. This award asks the institution to "demonstrate a commitment to the development of the candidate as a productive, independent investigator." Additionally, grant guidelines note that the NIH "...may begin requesting information essential to an assessment of the effectiveness of this program," including the recipient's "...employment history, publications, support from research grants or contracts, honors and awards, professional activities, and other information helpful in evaluating the impact of the program." In other words, the productivity of a grantee is judged to be an indicator of the quality of the mentoring received under the grant.

SUMMARY POINTS

➤ Funding organizations can play an important role in promoting the educational component of the research they fund. This role includes the support of career development and guidance to supplement scientific and technical training.

➤ One of the most frequent complaints from postdocs is the low level of compensation provided by funding organizations relative to the skills and experience of the postdoc.

➤ Many funding levels, especially in the life sciences, reflect the model pay scale used by the NIH for its NRSAs, which provide a stipend for first-year trainees of $26,256. The NIH and NSF should recognize that they have a de facto role in setting stipend levels that are followed by others and develop criteria by which to adjust these levels.

➤ The underlying assumption of most traineeships or fellowships is that the postdoctoral scholar receives, in addition to the stipend, both technical instruction and career guidance that can lead to improved abilities and career satisfaction in the future. Funding organizations can work toward ensuring that the acquisition of career skills and career development is indeed part of the postdoctoral experience.

➤ Most postdocs are paid directly as employees on a PIs research grant. The NIH and other funding organizations have few mechanisms to monitor the experience of these postdocs, and they tend to regard the administration of research grants as the institution's responsibility.

➤ Funding organizations can promote good oversight and guidance of postdocs through requests for mentoring information on proposal forms, promotion of mentoring committees, limits on the length of appointments, support for health care benefits, and support of teaching activities by postdocs.

7

The Postdoc and the Disciplinary Societies

The nation's disciplinary or professional societies[1] can play a larger role in enhancing the postdoctoral experience. Their membership affords a unique overview of broad fields, such as physics, mathematics, and chemistry, from which to collect and provide information.

In particular, advisers and postdocs need information about career opportunities beyond the laboratory. Web sites are effective mechanisms for describing society programs and providing information on an ongoing basis. A more focused forum is each society's annual meeting, where scientists and engineers at all levels gather to gain perspective, make contacts, and share information.

Meeting organizers can devise strategies to promote the professional careers of postdocs by, for example, placing them on the research program sessions so they receive the public exposure they deserve. Society meetings are also effective venues for bringing postdocs together with potential employers. The job search can be facilitated through formal presentations, informal drop-in rooms, and coffee sessions throughout the meeting. Funding agency representatives can discuss grant mechanisms and topics of high funding priority, allowing postdocs to gain perspective on grant possibilities.

Societies can take concrete steps to make the role of postdoctoral scholars more visible and to publicize the importance of that role. For example, they already provide travel funds that allow postdocs to attend their meetings; this practice could be expanded. In addition, they could invite postdocs to serve on

---

[1]Examples include the American Physical Society, the American Chemical Society, the American Geophysical Union, and the American Society for Microbiology.

95

their standing committees, where appropriate. They could award prizes to post-docs in which the role of the mentor might be highlighted. By focusing more attention on postdocs, they can increase the likelihood that advisers, institutions, and funding organizations will spend their own funds to send postdocs to meetings and take other steps to enrich the postdoctoral experience.

Professional societies can also translate their information and perspective into the development of norms regarding the postdoctoral experience. For example, they can suggest appropriate skills and standards that should be mastered by postdocs in particular disciplines prior to completion of their postdoctoral experience. They can, on the basis of their own or others' surveys and disciplinary knowledge, suggest standards for compensation, benefits, evaluations, or other practices that now vary widely.

Some disciplinary societies are active in collecting and analyzing information about the education, employment, compensation, distribution, trends, and other features of disciplinary life. This information can be useful for postdocs in planning their careers if it is made easily available (e.g., on the society's web site) and publicized in journals. Both postdocs and advisers can benefit from more information about new fields, subfields, and "hot" sectors of employment, both within and outside academia.

8

Principles, Action Points, and Recommendations for Enhancing the Postdoctoral Experience

In developing this guide, COSEPUP analyzed the gradually growing body of available data and information on postdocs, surveyed institutions that host postdoctoral scholars, met with 39 focus groups across the United States, and hosted a day-long workshop at the National Academies for all parties involved in the postdoctoral experience.

After reflecting on this information, the committee has concluded that most postdocs are gaining valuable research experiences and acquiring important laboratory and other research skills. However, the overall postdoctoral experience must encompass more than research experience if it is to fulfill its potential. Postdocs need better mentoring, better compensation, more information on employment opportunities, more assistance in planning their careers, and opportunities to learn a number of career skills (writing grant proposals, writing research papers, critiquing the papers or proposals of others, managing a small program or lab, mentoring or teaching students, and communicating to nonspecialists). The postdoc's need for career skills and educational experiences must be more widely recognized and reflected in all decisions made by postdoc advisers, host institutions, and the organizations that provide funding for postdocs.

The postdoc has a quid pro quo relationship with the research community. Postdocs have the obligation to carry out to the best of their ability the research program they have agreed to; the research community, in turn, has the obligation to provide the education, training, guidance, and experiences that lead to a successful and rewarding career.

COSEPUP concluded that there are significant opportunities to enhance the postdoctoral experience for the benefit of both the postdoctoral population and the research enterprise. This guide describes these opportunities in separate sets of recommendations for postdocs, advisers, institutions, funding organizations, and disciplinary societies. The three principles listed below provide the basis for these recommendations.

PRINCIPLES

1. *The postdoctoral experience is first and foremost a period of apprenticeship for the purpose of gaining scientific, technical, and other professional skills that advance the professional career.* Postdocs should not be viewed as just an inexpensive "pair of hands" in the laboratory. They should receive assistance in the development both of their scientific and technical skills and of other skills needed for a professional career. In this spirit, the term of a postdoc should not be greater than that needed to meet these education, training, and career development objectives.

2. *Postdocs should receive appropriate recognition (including lead author credit) and compensation (including health insurance and other fringe benefits) for the contribution they make to the research enterprise.* Postdoctoral research is a vital part of both the junior researchers career path and the research enterprise. Postdoctoral salaries should increase in accordance with years of experience so as to properly reflect the postdoc's level of education and skill. When a postdoc's contribution is thus valued and rewarded, a postdoctoral experience can (and should) be one of the most focused, productive, and exciting times in the career of a scientist or engineer.

3. *To ensure that postdoctoral appointments are beneficial to all concerned, all parties to the appointments—the postdoc, the postdoc adviser, the host institution, and funding organizations—should have a clear and mutually-agreed-upon understanding with regard to the nature and purpose of the appointment.* This understanding must include the objectives of the adviser and institution as well as the objectives of the postdoc. In addition, funding organizations have responsibilities to set high standards for the postdoctoral experience and the disciplinary societies have responsibilities to gather and disseminate information and promote career advancement. The quality of the postdoctoral experience is the responsibility of all.

The remainder of this chapter is devoted to the committee's recommendations, and is organized by target audience. Many of the recommendations include a rationale or other explanation. For those readers desiring a synopsis of the recommendations, the following summary of "action points" is provided.

ACTION POINTS

Advisers, institutions, funding organizations, and disciplinary societies should:

1. Award institutional recognition, status, and compensation commensurate with the postdocs' contributions to the research enterprise.

2. Develop distinct policies and standards for postdocs, modeled on those available for graduate students and faculty.

3. Develop mechanisms for frequent and regular communication between postdocs and their advisers, institutions, funding organizations, and disciplinary societies.

4. Monitor and provide formal evaluations (at least annually) of the performance of postdocs.

5. Ensure that all postdocs have access to health insurance, regardless of funding source, and to institutional services.

6. Set limits for total time as a postdoc (of approximately five years, summing time at all institutions), with clearly described exceptions as appropriate.

7. Invite the participation of postdocs when creating standards, definitions, and conditions for appointments.

8. Provide substantive career guidance to improve postdoc's ability to prepare for regular employment.

9. Improve the quality of data, both for postdoctoral working conditions and for the population of postdocs in relation to employment prospects in research.

10. Take steps to improve the transition of postdocs to regular career positions.

COSEPUP considered several other action points, but chose not to recommend them. These include measures to limit the postdoctoral population, to establish formal benchmarks for postdoc salaries, and to permit postdocs to obtain their own grant funding during the postdoctoral term. Because of the rapid pace of change in research institutions and the diversity of settings where postdocs work, the committee chose to avoid such fixed limits or measures. In addition, there is recent evidence that the postdoctoral population may be stabilizing in response to better information and opportunities in the nonacademic job market. Instead, COSEPUP urges graduate students, postdocs, advisers, institutions, funding agencies, and disciplinary societies to consider the following recommendations as they develop and apply their own policies.

RECOMMENDATIONS

Postdocs

1. *Postdocs should take responsibility for deciding whether to seek a post-doctoral position* and to define their objectives in doing so. Once they make this decision, they are responsible for informing themselves about what they can expect—and what is expected of them: the duration of the appointment, the expectations of the adviser, the institutional resources available, potential sources of financial support, institutional policies on authorship and intellectual property (including ownership of data, "tangible research material," such as antibodies, vaccines, etc.), and where to find information about careers in their particular field.

2. *Postdocs should contribute their best efforts to the program in which they work*, and consider themselves full members of that program as long as their appointment lasts.

3. *Postdocs share with their advisers the responsibility for frequent communication* in the interests of common understanding, productive research, and effective mentoring.

4. *Postdocs bear the primary responsibility for the success of their experience,* with the support of their advisers and institutions. Responsibilities include gaining new research skills, contributing to the effort of the lab or department, communicating with the adviser, initiating a network of colleagues, and concluding a research project in as timely a manner as possible.

Advisers

1. *The advisers of postdocs have the responsibility to provide a postdoctoral experience that is fundamentally educational in nature* and advances the postdoc's career. This educational experience should lead toward research independence and include, depending on the postdoc's career goals, occasional course work, teaching, internships, and other experiences that promote professional development.

2. At the outset of a postdoctoral appointment, *advisers should outline, in writing, the initial expectations about the performance of the postdoc*, including the overall research plan and the postdoc's responsibility for ongoing research. These understandings should include laboratory policies on authorship; on ownership of ideas, intellectual property, and data;

on determining priority of research projects; and, importantly, on taking projects from the laboratory when the postdoc's term has ended. This should be reviewed on an annual basis in case a mid-course correction is needed due to changes either in the adviser's assessment of the postdocs abilities or changes in the postdoc's career goals (see Recommendation 4).

3. In view of the role of the postdoc as a trainee, *the adviser should provide mentoring as needed*, including not only detailed advice and assistance in the development of a specific research project, but also education in research issues such as ethics and conflicts of interest.

4. *Advisers should discuss goals with the postdoc at the outset so the expectations of both parties are clearly delineated, and provide written evaluations of a postdoc's progress at least once a year,* to be included in the postdoc's institutional file. Such meetings provide an assessment and reality check for the postdoc and postdoc adviser.

5. *Advisers and departments should provide career counseling and job placement assistance.* They should also support the efforts of postdocs to gain experiences, compatible with their research responsibility, that will help prepare them for the job market.

6. *Advisers and departments should consider whether postdocs may benefit from additional mentoring by several members of an institution.* The purpose of such a mentoring committee would be to provide additional guidance and perspective to the postdoc, not to alter the important relation between postdoc and mentor.

Institutions

1. An important first step is for institutions to *take a census of their postdoctoral populations*. Many institutions, especially universities, have no accurate count or counting mechanism.

2. Institutions should *classify all postdocs in a distinctive and appropriate category that embraces their unique institutional position* (see Recommendation 1 in section on Funding Organizations). Classification as faculty or staff is not appropriate, because postdocs are apprentices; classification as students is not appropriate, because postdocs have completed the doctorate. Instead, they need a clear classification category that defines their standing and access to resources.

3. If they have not already done so, *institutions should establish explicit policies* regarding the appointment, training, compensation, benefits, evaluation, and career guidance of postdoctoral scholars.

4. In particular, *institutions should establish a minimum salary/stipend level for all postdocs.* Grant proposals should provide for regular increases in salary for postdocs, as they do for staff. All postdocs should also be provided with access to health insurance for themselves and their families.

5. *Institutions should adopt guidelines for the duration of postdoctoral terms.* Sometimes such terms may be exceeded under special circumstances (such as illness, birth or adoption of a child, a need for exposure to multiple fields, or a need to finish a project that has reached an advanced stage). The postdoctoral term should include time spent in postdoctoral positions at any previous institutions as well as at the present institution.

6. *There should be a general progression, as a postdoctoral term lengthens, toward more senior status*, with commensurate pay and benefits (see Recommendation 1 in section on Funding Organizations).

7. The institution should periodically *review the balance of interests among postdocs, advisers, departments, and the institution* in order to assure that the legitimate educational needs and career interests of postdocs are being met.

8. *Institutions should not encourage unlimited growth in the postdoctoral (or graduate student) population* in the face of limited employment opportunities. Many postdocs (and graduate students) are funded by federal grant mechanisms at least partly for the purpose of meeting investigators' needs for laboratory workers. An alternative is to increase the number of permanent laboratory workers.

9. *Institutions should maintain a postdoctoral office or officer* to provide guidance, logistical support, information on postdoctoral policies, opportunities for continuing education, and registration information for all postdocs. The institution should also designate an ombudsperson or other representative to provide counsel for postdocs (and advisers) and help arbitrate grievances.

10. *Institutions should encourage each of their divisions and programs to examine their roles in the education and training of postdocs and in maintaining high standards of mentoring.*

11. *Institutions should require evidence that funding for a postdoc is available before PIs are allowed to hire postdocs on research grants.*

12. *The institution should receive and keep on file a letter of appointment or contract* signed by the postdoc, adviser, and institutional representative. The letter should be accompanied by a statement of goals, policies, and responsibilities applicable to postdoctoral education, including the skills the postdoc should plan to develop to meet career objectives.

13. *The institution should ensure that postdocs have guidance in career planning.* If a career planning office exists, postdocs should have access to that office, ideally through an identified contact person who can provide specific assistance. Although the adviser plays the primary role in career advising, an institutional office may supplement this function in numerous ways, such as providing the opportunity for postdocs to participate in interviews with employers; programs in resume writing, interviewing, grant writing, and other appropriate subjects; inviting alumni and visiting speakers (including those from nonacademic settings) to discuss their careers; and providing information and materials.

14. *Institutions should ask advisers to prepare a written evaluation of their postdocs' progress/performance at least once a year.* This brief evaluation could consider such factors as research progress and next steps to be taken toward achieving career goals. In addition, institutions should encourage and provide opportunities for the postdoc to have multiple mentoring opportunities. Although some might question this activity as being too burdensome, if done properly it need not be extensive or time-consuming to have value. Examples include mentoring committees for each postdoc (analogous to a dissertation committee) and regular, informal presentations of research with feedback from lab members, senior scholars, and visiting researchers. Such evaluations, strongly desired by most postdocs, help avoid confusion about a postdoc's standing, build a more frank and open advising relationship, and provide a meaningful way for the adviser to compensate a postdoc for research performed.

15. *The special needs of foreign nationals should be addressed* by a contact person in an existing or new office of international services. This person should have expertise in visa and immigration policies.

16. *Each institution should encourage and financially support a post-doctoral association* that serves the social, informational, and logistical needs of postdocs and provides a mechanism for them to communicate with institutional leaders.

Funding Organizations

1. All organizations that provide funding for postdocs should ***work toward a definition of a postdoc*** that recognizes the temporary nature of the appointment and can be flexibly adapted to fit institutional systems of nomenclature. Such a definition would help avoid problems related to "the perennial postdoc," provide a better understanding of the number and nature of postdocs, and improve accountability for the use of funds. COSEPUP recommends that definitions reflect the following common distinction:

   a. PhDs who are in years 1-5 of their postdoctoral research (primarily a training phase);

   b. After five years, postdocs who are essential to the lab's productivity should be appointed as staff members in an appropriate staff category. Such research employees would also be eligible to apply for their own funding. Placement in a given category should generally be based on the total number of years a postdoc has worked at *all institutions* as postdocs. It should not be based on the number of years after the PhD (or other doctoral-level degree), because this measure would unfairly exclude those applicants who delayed postdocs for various reasons (e.g., starting families, disadvantaged financial background).

2. Each organization that provides funding for postdocs should have ***terms and conditions that apply to all postdocs supported by that funding.*** These terms and conditions should include the following:

   a. ***Appropriate salaries/stipends:*** Postdocs should receive stipends or salaries that are adequate and fairly adjusted to reflect their experience. If adequate compensation is not provided by the funding organization, the institution should appoint the postdoc only if supplementary funding is made available (see Recommendation 3e). Grant proposals should provide for regular increases in salary for postdocs, as they do for staff.

   b. ***Medical benefits:*** Postdocs should be provided with access to medical benefits for themselves and their families. Every effort should be made to normalize these benefits for all postdocs at an institution regardless of their individual sources of funding.

   c. ***Travel:*** Postdocs should have sufficient travel funding to attend at least one professional meeting each year.

   d. ***Leave:*** Postdocs should be governed by explicit leave policies, including sick leave, parental leave, and holidays.

   e. ***Performance reviews:*** Postdocs should receive regular performance reviews, both for the benefit of postdocs and so that the funding organization can better understand the quality and achievements of the postdocs they fund.

f. *Career planning:* Postdocs should receive career planning guidance at the institution where they work. In addition, funding organizations can themselves form or encourage the formation of postdoctoral and alumni associations where current and former postdocs can network regarding future employment.

g. *Career skill enhancement:* Postdocs, in consultation with their advisers, should be permitted to gain necessary extra-laboratory education and experiences that will enhance their skills development (e.g., teaching, class work) relative to the career they are pursuing. Advisers, institutions, and funding organizations must understand that such education and experiences are necessary to career development.

h. ***Reporting and tracking:*** Funding organizations should track postdocs after they leave individual labs, to help determine whether that lab should continue to receive funding for postdoc training; funders already use the yardstick of post-appointment performance for training grants. Tracking might be done via a web site, and should provide useful information, such as numbers, characteristics, and subsequent employment. When a postdoc experience ends, the organization can use a "virtual exit interview" (or some other mechanism) to determine the quality of a postdoc experience and to identify problems. Such reviews of outcomes may help federal organizations comply with the Government Performance and Results Act.

3. The ***NIH should establish*** a:

a. ***Central office for all postdocs:*** Currently, the management of the postdocs supported by NIH funding is spread throughout the NIH. Most postdocs are funded under research grants, far fewer by the training program, and fewer still by fellowship programs. As a result, no single entity tracks the status and needs of this growing population or responds directly to their concerns.

b. ***Stipend/salary scale for all postdocs:*** Regardless of its original purpose, many institutions use the NRSA postdoc stipend scale as the minimum for their postdocs. These relatively low stipends were originally designed not as salaries but as cost-sharing stipends for NRSA trainees to offset the cost of living during training. Despite its limited intention, this scale has become the de facto funding standard not only for NRSA trainees (a small fraction of the postdocs supported by the NIH) but also for biomedical postdocs in general, regardless of whether they are funded by a training program or by the NIH at all. A consequence (albeit unintended) is that many postdocs receive inadequate compensation. The NIH, working with the NSF and other federal agencies, should develop rational criteria for a pay scale or guideline for postdocs. Such a scale or guideline should be reviewed regularly. Also, any scale must be instituted both prospectively and retrospectively. Currently, NIH increases its stipend levels annually without supplementing existing grants, which leads to inequities.

c.   ***Standard postdoc definition***: See Recommendation 1, above. This is particularly important for the NIH where the common use of "research associate" does not differentiate postdocs from non-PhD researchers or others who may work in the same laboratories.

d.   ***Annual meetings with postdoc representatives***: Postdocs, especially those supported on research grants, may have little or no contact with their funding organization. The NIH leadership should meet regularly with representatives of postdoctoral organizations to provide a direct communication link between the funding agencies and postdoctoral associations (and the national network of associations being formed).

e.   ***Allow institutions and PIs the ability to combine the funding from the traineeship program and from NIH research grants so the PI may increase the stipend for postdocs without requiring an increase in the number of hours a postdoc must work.*** Currently, the NIH does not allow supplementation of NRSAs from research grants. In this situation and in others where supplementation is not allowed, a pooled system would introduce new flexibility to setting stipend levels. If PIs were allowed to supplement NRSAs, who are highly desirable contributors to the research process, the law of supply and demand might raise compensation levels in general. Raising salaries could slightly reduce the total number of postdocs, but higher pay could also increase postdocs' status and focus greater attention on their training, productivity, and evaluation.

4. The ***NSF should establish*** a:
   a.   ***Central office responsible for all postdocs***: Like the NIH, no single office at the NSF follows postdocs (although there is an office for graduate students). In most cases, the postdocs are funded under research grants from the directorates, and in only a very small number of cases by fellowship programs. Postdocs need an informed person or office with whom to discuss concerns and, when necessary, grievances.

   b.   ***Stipend/salary scale for all postdocs***: See Recommendation 3b, above. The NSF should create a clear rationale for setting the stipend/ salary for postdocs funded on NSF grants—even for those funded by fellowship programs—and review the pay scale regularly.

   c.   ***Improved definition of a postdoc***: See Recommendation 1, above.

The NSF defines a postdoc on its grant proposals as an "individual within five years of their PhD." However, this definition does not apply to all postdocs nor, as noted above, does the use of a fixed number of years allow for valid exceptions due to various personal situations.

d. *Annual meetings with postdoc representatives*: Postdocs funded under NSF research grants have no communication link with the organization that funds them. NSF leaders should meet regularly with representatives of postdoctoral associations (and perhaps the national network of associations being formed) to facilitate communication with postdocs generally.

e. *A policy for the NSF's Division of Science Resource Studies to gather data regularly for postdocs, as it does for graduate students.* Underrepresented US minorities and women should receive particular attention, given a falloff in their participation in science and engineering after graduate school.

5. *Private funding organizations, such as foundations, should play a larger role in encouraging best practices and setting appropriate stipend levels.* Foundations can make the enhancement of the overall quality of the postdoctoral experience a top priority and encourage other foundations to do the same. In addition, they can be instrumental in convening postdocs for small professional and information meetings.

6. *Non-governmental organizations and foreign governments should assume their own responsibilities for postdocs.* Those non-governmental organizations or foreign governments that provide postdocs with low or partial funding should recognize that host institutions might not supplement these low stipends/salaries. Such organizations should require supplemental funding as a condition of awarding such a fellowship and/or reduce the number of postdocs funded in order to raise the stipend/salary to an appropriate level.

7. *Funding organizations should require that those seeking to support postdocs under training or research grants demonstrate their qualifications for this responsibility.* For example, they could be required (as is now sometimes the case for graduate students) to list their previous postdocs, what those postdocs have published, and where they are currently are employed.

8. COSEPUP supports the following recommendation from the *Trends* report: "Because of its concern for optimizing the creativity of young scientists and broadening the variety of scientific problems under study

in the life sciences, the committee recommends that public and private funding agencies establish *'career-transition' grants* for senior postdoctoral fellows. The intent is to identify the highest-quality scientists while they are still postdoctoral fellows and give them the financial independence to begin new scientific projects of their own design in anticipation of their obtaining fully independent positions."[1]

Disciplinary Societies

1. *Disciplinary societies should play a larger role in promoting the professional careers of postdocs,* especially by enhancing opportunities at professional society meetings. These opportunities include placing postdocs on the scientific program so they receive public exposure, providing travel grant support to attend meetings, inviting postdocs to serve on standing committees of the organization, sponsoring workshops for potential postdocs at major professional meetings, and inviting representatives from funding agencies to discuss funding mechanisms and issues.

2. *Disciplinary societies should support job searches by postdocs,* both by maintaining job lists and web sites, and by introducing postdocs to prospective employers, especially at annual meetings. They should invite outside groups to present information at their meetings, especially information about nonacademic and nonresearch careers.

3. *Disciplinary societies should develop norms* regarding the postdoctoral experience in their field that could be adopted by advisers and institutions in their field.

4. *Disciplinary societies should collect and analyze data and provide the best available information about career planning and employment prospects* for postdocs in their field. They should inform prospective postdocs (including beginning graduate students) about market demand and other issues of interest to those entering a research-focused profession. They might supplement or advance the practice by institutions and funding organizations of tracking postdocs through their careers.

5. *Disciplinary societies should organize programs or workshops to advance professional skills.* Topics might include grant writing, communication, CV preparation, and writing cover letters. Such programs could also offer junior researchers the chance to network with senior colleagues.

---

[1]*Trends in the Early Career of Life Scientists,* p. 85

6. ***Each disciplinary society should examine the purpose of the post-doctoral experience for its discipline,*** and ask the following question: What are the professional standards that our discipline demands at the end of the postdoctoral experience? Each society should be proactive in striving to have those standards met. Such standards could perhaps determine whether a postdoc progresses from associate membership to full membership in the society.

LOOKING TOWARD THE FUTURE

The theme underlying this guide is that all parties to the postdoctoral experience—postdocs, advisers, institutions, funding organizations, and disciplinary societies—must reach a clear, mutual understanding of the purpose of a post-doctoral position. Once such an understanding is gained, all parties can work together to enhance the postdoctoral experience. COSEPUP hopes this guide will help them to do so.

Bibliography

Abbot, A., and G. Stiegler. 1996. Careers and Recruitment: The View From Europe. *Nature* 383: 199-200.

American Association for the Advancement of Science. Science's Next Wave Forum: The Situation of Postdocs; available on-line at (http://www.nextwave.org/discussions/).

American Association for the Advancement of Science. 1995. *Science Careers '95: The Future of the PhD* 270: 121-146.

American Chemical Society. 1995. *Employment Patterns of Recent Doctorates in Chemistry: Institutional Perspectives and Imperatives for Change.* The Presidential Task Force on the Study of Doctoral Education in Chemistry. Washington, DC: American Chemical Society.

American Institute of Physics. 1996. *Underemployment Among Postdoctorates: 1994 Society Membership Survey.* Education and Employment Statistics Division. College Park, MD: American Institute of Physics.

Ammons, S. 1996. Association of American Medical Colleges. *Survey of PhD Students in U.S. Medical Schools, 1994-1995.*

Assmus, A. 1993. The Creation of Postdoctoral Fellowships and the Siting of American Scientific Research. *Minerva* 31(2): 150-183.

Association of American Universities. 1998. *Graduate Education Report: Final Draft.* Washington DC: Association of American Universities.

Association of American Universities. 1998. *Report and Recommendations.* Committee on Postdoctoral Education. Washington, DC: Association of American Universities.

Bauer, E. 1993. Reforming Physics and Physicists for Lean Times [Letter to the editor]. *Physics Today* 46:11.

Breneman, D. W. 1975. *Graduate School Adjustments to the 'New Depression' in Higher Education.* National Board on Graduate Education Technical Report No. 3. Washington, DC: National Academy of Sciences.

Bunk, S. 1998. Fewer Academic Jobs Spur Postdocs to Organize Against Disadvantages. *The Scientist* 12(1):1.

110

COSEPUP (Committee on Science, Engineering, and Public Policy). 1995. *On Being a Scientist: Responsible Conduct in Research.* Washington, DC: National Academy Press; available on-line at (www.nap.edu).

COSEPUP (Committee on Science, Engineering, and Public Policy). 1995. *Reshaping the Graduate Education of Scientists and Engineers.* Washington, DC: National Academy Press.

COSEPUP (Committee on Science, Engineering, and Public Policy). 1996. *A National Conversation on Doctoral Education, and Emerging Consensus.* Washington, DC: National Academy Press; available on-line at (http://www4.nas.edu/pd/convo.nsf).

COSEPUP (Committee on Science, Engineering, and Public Policy). 1996. *Careers in Science and Engineering: A Student Planning Guide to Grad School and Beyond.* Washington, DC: National Academy Press; available on-line at (http://www.nap.edu/readingroom/books/careers/).

COSEPUP (Committee on Science, Engineering, and Public Policy). 1997. *Adviser, Teacher, Role Model, Friend: On Being a Mentor to Students in Science and Engineering.* Washington, DC: National Academy Press; available on-line at (www.nap.edu/readingroom/books/mentor).

Doering, D. 1995. Degrees of Freedom. *Science* 269:903.

Fechter, A. E., and C.D. Gaddy. 1998. Trends in Doctoral Education and Employment. *Higher Education: Handbook of Theory and Research* (13). New York: Agathon Press.

Garrison, H., and P. Brown. 1986. *The Career Achievements of NIH Postdoctoral Trainees and Fellows.* Committee on National Needs for Biomedical and Behavioral Research Personnel, Institute of Medicine. Washington, DC: National Academy Press.

Hays, S. L. 1996. *At the Edge of a New Frontier: A Profile of the Stanford University Biomedical PhD Class of 1996 and Recommendations for the Future: A Biomass (Biomedical Association of Stanford Students) Report.* Stanford, CA: Stanford University.

Henderson, P.H., J.E. Clark, and M.A. Reynolds. 1996. *Summary Report 1995: Doctorate Recipients from United States Universities.* Washington, DC: National Academy Press.

Knox, J. 1996. The Evolving World of the Post-doctoral Research Scientist. *National Forum Magazine* (Fall); available on-line at (http://www.auburn.edu/academic/societies/phi_kappa_phi/natforum.html.).

Kuh, C. 1995. *Comments on the Usefulness of the Massy/Goldman Study in Formulation of National Policy Concerning the Graduate Education of Scientists and Engineers.* Educational Testing Service Discussion Paper. Princeton, NJ: Educational Testing Service.

Massy, W. and G. Goldman. 1995. *The Production and Utilization of Science and Engineering Doctorates in the US.* Palo Alto, CA: Stanford University.

McPheron M., and Nerad M. 1999. Results of a Survey of Postdoctoral Appointees at UC Berkeley. University of California, Berkeley.

Mervis, J. 1996. NSF to Take Closer Look at How Support Shapes Careers. *Science* 272:806.

Nerad M., and J. Cerny. 1999. Postdoctoral Patterns, Career Advancement, and Problems. *Science* 285: 1533-5.

NRC (National Research Council). 1981. *Postdoctoral Appointments and Disappointments.* Washington, DC: National Academy Press.

NRC (National Research Council). 1992. *Educating Mathematical Scientists: Doctoral Study and the Postdoctoral Experience in the United States.* Washington, DC: National Academy Press.

NRC (National Research Council). 1994. *The Funding of Young Investigators in the Biological and Biomedical Sciences.* Washington, DC: National Academy Press

NRC (National Research Council). 1998. *Trends in the Early Careers of Life Scientists.* Washington DC: National Academy Press.

NSF (National Science Foundation, Division of Science Resources Studies). 1993. *Academic Science/ Engineering: Graduate Enrollment and Support, Fall 1991.* Washington, DC: NSF.

NSF (National Science Foundation). 1995. *Graduate Education and Postdoctoral Training in the Mathematical and Physical Sciences.* NSF 96-30. Arlington, VA: NSF.

NSF (National Science Foundation, Division of Science Resources Studies). 1995. *Selected Data on Graduate Students and Postdoctorates in Science and Engineering: Fall 1993 Selected Data Tables.* Arlington, VA: NSF.

NSF (National Science Foundation). 1996. *Characteristics of Doctoral Scientists and Engineers in the United States: 1993.* NSF 96-302. Arlington, VA: NSF.

NSF (National Science Foundation). 1996. *Selected Data on Science and Engineering Doctorate Awards* NSF 96-303. Arlington, VA: NSF.

OECD (Organisation for Economic Co-operation and Development). 1995. *Research Training: Present & Future.* Paris, France: OCED.

OSEP (Office of Scientific and Engineering Personnel, National Research Council). 1998. *Trends in the Early Careers of Life Scientists.* Washington, DC: National Academy Press.

Radetsky, P. 1994. The Modern Postdoc: Prepping for the Job Market. *Science* 265: 1909-1910.

Regets, M. 1998. *Has the Use of Postdocs Changed?.* National Science Foundation, Division of Science Resources Studies, Issue Brief. NSF 99-310, 1998.

Ries, P. 1994. *Assessment of National Data Sources.* Unpublished Working Paper, National Research Council.

Sample, S. B. 1993. *Postdoctoral Education in America.* Address Before the Annual Meeting of the Association of Graduate Schools, Chapel Hill, NC, September 23.

Swinbanks, D. 1996. Postdoctoral Positions Galore in Japan. *Nature* 383: 200.

Syverson, P. D. 1994. Postdoctoral Education Back in the Limelight. *Communicator* (April): 9-11.

Tobias, S., D.E. Chubin, and K. Aylesworth. 1996. Chutes and Ladders: In an Unstable Market for New Ph.D's, Success in Science Must be Redefined to Include Careers Outside the Ivory Tower. *The Sciences* 36(4): 17-21.

University of California, Council on Graduate Deans. 1998. Report on Postdoctoral Education at UC, Fall 1998; available on-line at (www.ogsr.ucsd.edu/PostdocEdu/Report.html).

Van Ryzin, G., S. Dietz, J. Winer, and D. Wright. 1996. *The Employment Outlook in the Microbiological Sciences: Prepared for American Society for Microbiology.* Rockville, MD: Westat, Inc.

Vogel, G. 1999. *Science* 285: 1531.

Zumeta, W. 1984. Anatomy of the Boom in Postdoctoral Appointments During the 1970s: Troubling Implications for Quality Science? *Science, Technology, & Human Values* 9(2): 23-37.

Zumeta, W. 1985. *Extending the Educational Ladder: The Changing Quality and Value of Postdoctoral Study.* Lexington, MA: DC Heath and Company.

Zumeta, W. 1998. State Higher Education Finance and Policy Developments: 1997. *The NEA 1998 Almanac of Higher Education.* Washington, DC: National Education Association.

Note: Relevant web sites are at COSEPUP's Postdoctoral Web site at www.nationalacademies.org/postdocs.

Appendixes

Appendix A

Committee on Science, Engineering, and Public Policy: Member and Staff Biographical Information

Maxine F. Singer (*Chair*), president of the Carnegie Institution of Washington (Washington, DC), is an eminent biochemist whose wide-ranging research on RNA and DNA has greatly advanced scientific understanding of viral and human genes. Dr. Singer received her bachelor's degree from Swarthmore College (1952) and her PhD from Yale University (1957). She worked at the National Institutes of Health as a research biochemist in the National Institute of Arthritis and Metabolic Diseases until 1975, studying the synthesis and structure of RNA. In 1975 she moved to the National Cancer Institute. Her interest in primate DNA led to the discovery of a transposable element in the human genome. A member of the National Academy of Sciences and the Institute of Medicine, she currently serves on the Board of Directors of the Weizmann Institute and the Johnson & Johnson Corporation. She received the Distinguished Presidential Rank Award, the highest honor given to a civil servant, and the National Medal of Science in 1991.

Bruce M. Alberts, president of the National Academy of Sciences, is a respected biochemist recognized for his work in biochemistry and molecular biology. He is noted particularly for his extensive study of the protein complexes that allow chromosomes to be replicated, as required for a living cell to divide. He is a past chair of the Commission on Life Sciences and has served on the faculty of Princeton University and as vice chair and chair of the Department of Biochemistry and Biophysics of the University of California, San Francisco. Being committed to the improvement of science education, he has dedicated much of his time to education projects in San Francisco elementary schools.

115

Enriqueta C. Bond received her undergraduate degree in zoology and physiology from Wellesley College, a master's degree in biology and genetics from the University of Virginia, and a PhD in molecular biology and biochemical genetics from Georgetown University. She is a member of the American Association for the Advancement of Science, the American Society for Microbiology, and the American Public Health Association. She serves on the Board of Health Sciences Policy of the Institute of Medicine (IOM), the Board of the Society for the Advancement of Research on Women's Health, and the Board of the North Carolina Biotechnology Center. Dr. Bond was executive officer of IOM from 1989 to 1994. She became president of the Burroughs Wellcome Fund in July 1994.

Lewis M. Branscomb is the Aetna Professor of Public Policy and Corporate Management emeritus and former director of the Science, Technology, and Public Policy Program in the Center for Science and International Affairs at Harvard University's Kennedy School of Government. Dr. Branscomb graduated from Duke University in 1945, summa cum laude, and was awarded a PhD in physics by Harvard University in 1949. He has held teaching positions at the University of Maryland and the University of Colorado. He is a former president of the American Physical Society and of Sigma Xi, the Scientific Research Society. A research physicist at the National Bureau of Standards (now the National Institute of Standards and Technology) from 1951-1969, he was its director from 1969-1972. He is a member of the National Academy of Engineering, the National Academy of Sciences, the Institute of Medicine, and the National Academy of Public Administration. He serves on the Technology Assessment Advisory Committee to the Technology Assessment Board of the US Congress. Dr. Branscomb is a former director of the IBM Europe, Middle East, Africa Corporation and of General Foods Corporation. He is a director of Mobil, MITRE, and the Lord Corporation and C.S. Draper Laboratories. He has written extensively on science and technology policy, comparative science and technology policy of different nations, information technology, management of technology, and atomic and molecular physics.

Peter Diamond is an Institute Professor and Professor of Economics at the Massachusetts Institute of Technology (MIT), where he has taught since 1966. He received his BA in mathematics from Yale University in 1960 and his PhD in economics from MIT in 1963. He has been president and chair of the National Academy of Social Insurance (NASI), president of the Econometric Society, and vice president of the American Economic Association. He is a fellow of the American Academy of Arts and Sciences and a member of the National Academy of Sciences. He was the recipient of the 1980 Mahalanobis Memorial Award and the 1994 Nemmers Prize. He has written on public finance, social insurance, uncertainty and search theories, and macroeconomics.

Gerald P. Dinneen was foreign secretary of the National Academy of Engineering from 1988 to 1995. He was previously vice president of science and technology at Honeywell Corporation and, from 1977-1981, was the assistant secretary of defense and principal deputy under secretary of defense for research and engineering. He has had a long affiliation with the Massachusetts Institute of Technology (MIT) having joined the MIT Lincoln Laboratory in Lexington, MA, in 1953. He advanced through many positions to become director from 1970-1977 and professor of electrical engineering from 1971-1981. He was elected to the National Academy of Engineering in 1975 and serves on many advisory committees and boards in the National Research Council and in government. He has been elected to the Engineering Academy of Japan, the Swiss Academy of Technological Sciences, and the Royal Academy of Engineering of the UK.

Mildred S. Dresselhaus is an Institute Professor of Electrical Engineering and Physics at the Massachusetts Institute of Technology. She has been active in the study of a wide array of problems in the physics of solids, and recently has been studying carbon nanotubes and other nanostructures. She was awarded the National Medal of Science in November 1990 and was elected to the National Academy of Engineering in 1974 and to the National Academy of Sciences (NAS) in 1985. She has been a member of the councils of both academies and of the Governing Board of the National Research Council, treasurer of NAS, and president of the American Physical Society and of the American Association for the Advancement of Science.

James J. Duderstadt is president emeritus and University Professor of Science and Engineering at the University of Michigan. He received his BA from Yale University in 1964 and his doctorate in engineering science and physics from the California Institute of Technology in 1967. He joined the faculty of the University of Michigan in 1968 and has served as professor of nuclear engineering, dean of the College of Engineering, provost, vice president for academic affairs, and president from 1984-1996. He received the National Medal of Technology for exemplary service to the nation, the E.O. Lawrence Award for excellence in nuclear research, and the Arthur Holly Compton Prize for outstanding teaching. He has served as chair of the National Science Board, chair of the Board of Directors of the Big Ten Athletic Conference, and chair of the Executive Board of the University of Michigan's hospitals. He serves as a director of the Unisys Corporation and CMS Energy Corporation. He has been a member of the National Academy of Engineering since 1987.

Marye Anne Fox is a chemist, a member of the National Academy of Sciences (NAS), and North Carolina State University's twelfth chancellor. Her research interests include physical organic chemistry, organic photochemistry, organic electrochemistry, chemical reactivity in non-homogeneous systems, heterogeneous photocatalysis, and electronic transfer in anisotropic macromolecular arrays. She has served on the Council of the NAS, its Executive Committee, and its Committee on Science and Education Policy. She has served as vice chair of the National Science Board (1994-1996) and chaired its Committee on Programs and Plans (1991-1994). She has served on the Texas Governor's Science and Technology Council and numerous community-based boards and has chaired the Chemistry Section of the American Association for the Advancement of Science, where she advises its Center for Science, Technology, and the Congress. She serves on boards for the North Carolina Microelectronics Center, Research Triangle Institute, and North Carolina Arboretum.

Ralph E. Gomory has been president of the Alfred P. Sloan Foundation since 1989. After having been a Higgins Lecturer and assistant professor at Princeton, he joined IBM in 1959, became vice president in 1973, and was senior vice president for science and technology in 1985-1989. A member of both the National Academy of Sciences and the National Academy of Engineering, he has received the Lanchester Prize in 1963, the John von Neumann Theory Prize in 1984, the IEEE Engineering Leadership Recognition Award in 1988, the National Medal of Science in 1988, the Arthur M. Bueche Award of the National Academy of Engineering in 1993, and the Heinz Award for Technology, the Economy, and Employment in 1998. He was named to the President's Council of Advisors on Science and Technology in 1990 and served to March 1993.

Ruby P. Hearn is senior vice president of the Robert Wood Johnson Foundation, which has awarded over $2 billion in grant funds since its inception as a national philanthropy in 1972. As a member of the executive management team, she participates in strategic program planning with the president and executive vice president and serves as a special adviser to the president and as the foundation's liaison in the nonprofit community. Dr. Hearn has had the major responsibility for oversight and program development of initiatives in maternal, infant, and child health, AIDS, substance abuse, and minority-group medical education. She received her MS and PhD in biophysics from Yale University and is a graduate of Skidmore College. She is a fellow of the Yale Corporation. She served on the Executive Committee of the Board of Directors for the 1995 Special Olympics World Summer Games in Connecticut. She is a member of the Institute of Medicine and its Council, COSEPUP, the Board of Directors of the Council on Foundations, the Science Board of the Food and Drug Administration, and the Advisory Committee to the Director of the National Institutes of Health.

Brigid L.M. Hogan is an investigator with the Howard Hughes Medical Institute and Hortense B. Ingram Professor in the Department of Cell Biology at Vanderbilt University School of Medicine. She obtained her PhD from Cambridge University, England, and carried out postdoctoral training at the Massachusetts Institute of Technology. Before moving to the United States, she was head of the Laboratory of Molecular Embryology, first at the Imperial Cancer Research Fund and then at the National Institute of Medical Research in London. Dr. Hogan is a member of the European Molecular Biology Organization and the Institute of Medicine.

Samuel H. Preston became dean of the University of Pennsylvania School of Arts and Sciences in January 1998 and has been a faculty member in sociology since 1979. He is a scholar of population studies with expertise in technical demography and the analysis of mortality and family structure. He has served twice as chair of the Department of Sociology, three times as chair of the Graduate Group in Demography, and as director of the Population Studies Center and Population Aging Research Center. Dr. Preston is a member of the National Academy of Sciences, the Institute of Medicine, the American Academy of Arts and Sciences, the American Association for the Advancement of Science, and the American Philosophical Society. Earlier in his career he served as a faculty member at the University of California at Berkeley and at the University of Washington. He was acting chief of the Population Trends and Structure Section of the UN Population Division from 1977-1979. Dr. Preston holds a BA from Amherst College and a PhD in economics from Princeton University.

Kenneth I. Shine is president of the Institute of Medicine and professor of medicine emeritus at the University of California, Los Angeles (UCLA) School of Medicine. At the UCLA School of Medicine, he was dean and provost for medical services. He has also been director of the Coronary Care Unit, chief of the Cardiology Division, and chair of the Department of Medicine at the UCLA School of Medicine. He has served as chair of the Council of Deans of the Association of American Medical Colleges, and was president of the American Heart Association. His research interests include metabolic events in the heart muscle, the relation of behavior to heart disease, and emergency medicine.

Morris Tanenbaum was the vice chair of the board and chief financial officer of AT&T from 1988-1991. He began his career at Bell Telephone Labs on the technical staff and held various positions at Western Electric Company, including vice president of the Engineering Division and vice president of manufacturing, before returning to Bell Labs in 1975 as executive vice president. In 1978 he became president of New Jersey Bell Telephone Company. He returned to AT&T as executive vice president for Corporate Affairs and planning in 1980, and became the first chair and CEO of AT&T Communications in 1984. He was vice president of the National Academy of Engineering until June 1998.

Irving L. Weissman is Karele and Avice Beekhuis Professor of Cancer Biology, professor of pathology, and professor of developmental biology at Stanford

University School of Medicine. Dr. Weissman was a member of the Scientific Advisory Board of Amgen (1981-1989), DNAX (1981-1992), and T-Cell Sciences (1988-1992). He was a co-founder of SyStemix and was chairman of its Scientific Advisory Board and a member of its Board of Directors in 1988-1997. His main research interests are hematopoietic stem cells, lymphocyte differentiation, lymphocyte homing receptors, and phylogeny of the immune system.

Sheila E. Widnall received her BSc (1960), MS (1961), and ScD (1964) in aeronautics and astronautics from the Massachusetts Institute of Technology (MIT). She was appointed Rockefeller Mauze Professor of Aeronautics and Astronautics at MIT in 1986 and served as MIT's associate provost from 1992-1993. After serving as secretary of the US Air Force from 1993-1997 she returned to her faculty position at MIT.

William Julius Wilson is the Lewis P. and Linda L. Geyser University Professor at Harvard University. He was formerly Lucy Flower University Professor of Sociology and Public Policy at the University of Chicago. He received the National Medal of Science in 1998. He is a member of the National Academy of Sciences, the American Academy of Arts and Sciences, and the National Academy of Education; a former member of the President's Committee on the National Medal of Science; and a past president of both the American Sociological Association and the Consortium of Social Science Associations.

William A. Wulf is president of the National Academy of Engineering (NAE). He was AT&T Professor of Engineering and Applied Science at the University of Virginia. He has served as assistant director of the National Science Foundation, chairman and CEO of Tartan Laboratories, Inc., and professor of computer science at Carnegie Mellon University. He has been a member of NAE since 1993 and served as chair of the Computer Science and Telecommunications Board.

Staff

Richard E. Bissell is executive director of the Policy Division of the National Academy of Sciences and Director of COSEPUP. He took up his current position in June 1998. Most recently, he served as coordinator of the Interim Secretariat of the World Commission on Dams (1997-1998) and as a member and chair of the Inspection Panel at the World Bank (1994-1997). He worked closely with the National Academy of Sciences during his tenure in senior positions at the US Agency for International Development (1986-1993) and as head of both the Bureau of Science and Technology and the Bureau of Program and Policy Coordination. He has published widely in political economy and has taught at Georgetown University and the University of Pennsylvania. He received his BA from Stanford University (1968) and his MA and PhD from Tufts University (1970, 1973).

Deborah D. Stine is associate director of COSEPUP, director of the Office of Special Projects, and director of the National Academies Christine Mirzayan Internship Program. She has worked on various projects in the National Academies since 1989. She received a National Research Council group award for her first study for COSEPUP, on policy implications of greenhouse warming, and a Commission on Life Sciences staff citation for her work in risk assessment and management. She holds a bachelor's degree in mechanical and environmental engineering from the University of California, Irvine; a master's degree in business administration from Texas A&M; and a PhD in public administration, specializing in policy analysis, from the American University. Before coming to the National Academies, she was a mathematician for the US Air Force, an air-pollution engineer for the state of Texas, and an air-issues manager for the Chemical Manufacturers Association.

Appendix B

Analysis of Quantitative Data on Postdocs

T he amount of data available on postdoctoral scholars in science and engineering is quite limited compared to that available for graduate students. For example, the number of graduate students funded by agency and funding mechanisms is known (such as how many graduate students are supported by NIH via both fellowships and research grants), but the same is not true for postdoctoral scholars.

Provided in this appendix is all the available quantitative data COSEPUP was able to locate on postdoctoral scholars. The data provided here in tables is also illustrated in figures throughout the text.

The surveys, sponsored by the National Science Foundation (NSF), which serve as the basis for the tables and figures in the text are the:

- Survey of Earned Doctorates (SED), which is a census of all doctorates awarded by US educational institutions;
- Survey of Doctorate Recipients (SDR), which is a biennial sample survey drawn from the SED;
- Survey of Graduate Students and Postdoctorates in Science and Engineering, which is an annual survey of the academic departments of all post-baccalaureate institutions.

Note that the use of NSF data does not imply NSF endorsement of the research methods or conclusions contained in this report.

The following is a brief description of the assumptions and restrictions used to extract information from the individual data files.

SURVEY OF EARNED DOCTORATES (SED)
(1920-1998)

The specialties list used in the SED for identifying doctoral fields in Science and Engineering (S&E) consists of the following major categories:

- Agricultural Sciences
- Biological Sciences
- Health Sciences
- Engineering
- Computer and Information Sciences
- Mathematics
- Physical Sciences
- Astronomy
- Atmospheric Sciences and Meteorology
- Chemistry
- Geological & Related Sciences
- Physics
- Miscellaneous Physical Sciences
- Psychology
- Social Sciences

For the purpose of this guide these names were used to identify fields or they were combined as follows:

- Life Sciences (Agricultural Sciences, Biological Sciences, Health Sciences)
- Engineering
- Mathematical Sciences (Computer and Information Sciences, Mathematics)
- Physics and Astronomy (Physics, Astronomy)
- Earth, Atmospheric, and Ocean Sciences (Atmospheric Sciences and Meteorology, Geological & Related Sciences, Miscellaneous Physical Sciences [except Other Physical Sciences])
- Chemistry
- Social and Behavioral Sciences (Psychology, Social Sciences)

All doctorates were selected independent of citizenship in determining the number of doctorates by field and in identifying postdoctoral plans in Table B-11. Only those doctorates who indicated that they have accepted a postdoctoral position or are negotiating with a specific organization were selected.

SURVEY OF DOCTORATE RECIPIENTS (SDR)
(1973-1997)

In using the SDR data set, the same doctoral field identifiers were used as those for the Doctorate Recipient File (DRF). Median salaries were determined only for a six-year cohort, 1991-1996, of doctorates that in 1997 identified themselves as being in a postdoctoral position and only for fields where a sufficient number of responses would provide reliable information. For the other figures using the SDR data, no restriction to a particular cohort was used. Data for Figure 3-2 was generated for married individuals in the year of the survey and for married individuals with children of any age under 18. Figure 1-7, containing information on the reasons why individuals were in a postdoctoral position, pertains to their current position; two categories, "additional training" and "postdoc is excepted," were combined into a single category. Figure 2-4, which reported the employment status of 1995 postdoctoral appointees in 1997, was obtained by merging the 1995 and 1997 data to obtain responses for individuals who responded to both surveys. Figure 1-5 provides data on the median number of years individuals are in postdoctoral positions by doctoral field, and this data was available only for the 1995 survey year as a special module for the survey.

SURVEY OF GRADUATE STUDENTS AND POSTDOCTORATES IN
SCIENCE AND ENGINEERING
(1973-1998)

The field taxonomy for this survey is slightly different from that of the SDR or DRF since it is a survey of graduate departments and not research fields. The following departmental identifiers or a subset of those departments were used for this analysis:

- Agricultural Sciences
- Biological Sciences
- Health Fields
- Engineering
- Mathematics and Computer Sciences
- Chemistry
- Earth, Atmospheric, and Ocean Sciences
- Physics and Astronomy
- Psychology
- Social Sciences

This data was extracted from the National Science Foundation's CASPER Data System. Categories were selected from menus provided by the system. Figure 1-2 contains data on all individuals holding a postdoctoral position, independent of citizenship, and whether they received a PhD or a professional degree (MD, DO, DVM, or DDS). Figure 2-5 distinguishes postdoctoral appointments by citizenship, and permanent residents are counted as US citizens. All other figures and tables using data from the Survey of Graduate Students and Post-doctorates in Science and Engineering made no restrictions as to citizenship or type of doctorate.

A DESCRIPTION OF THE DEGREE FIELD

A broad and fine degree taxonomy was used to describe the doctoral fields in this Guide. The following is a list of the broad field headings with the fine fields that comprise that broad field under its heading.

Life Sciences
    Agricultural Sciences
    Biological Sciences (includes Biochemistry)
    Medical Sciences

Engineering

Mathematical and Computer Sciences
    Computer Sciences
    Mathematical Sciences

Physical Sciences
    Physics and Astronomy
    Chemistry (does not include Biochemistry)
    Earth, Atmospheric, and Ocean Sciences

Social and Behavioral Sciences
    Social Sciences
    Psychology

LIST OF TABLES

TABLE B-1: Postdoctoral Appointees in Academic Institutions by Broad Field, 1980-1998

	1980	1981	1982	1983	1984	1985	1986	1987	1988	1989
Life Sciences	11,721	12,836	12,703	13,699	14,421	14,958	15,920	16,874	17,540	18,984
Physical Sciences and Mathematics	4,796	4,971	4,379	5,128	5,163	5,214	5,556	5,724	6,077	6,128
Engineering	979	1,033	978	1,107	1,202	1,355	1,402	1,444	1,688	1,917
Social and Behavioral Sciences	904	790	804	779	749	860	843	839	818	903
All Science &Engineering Fields	18,400	19,635	19,364	20,713	21,535	22,387	23,721	24,881	26,123	27,932

	1990	1991	1992	1993	1994	1995	1996	1997	1998
Life Sciences	20,214	21,051	22,671	24,158	25,704	25,144	26,119	26,836	28,283
Physical Sciences and Mathematics	6,506	6,673	6,830	6,822	7,132	7,183	7,276	7,495	7,511
Engineering	1,943	2,254	2,360	2,443	2,600	2,641	2,674	2,951	2,830
Social and Behavioral Sciences	902	887	385	899	941	958	1,038	936	995
All Science & Engineering Fields	29,565	30,865	32,747	34,322	36,377	35,926	37,107	38,218	39,619

Source: Survey of Graduate Students and Postdoctorates in Science and Engineering, 1980-1998

Note: Life Sciences includes the Agricultural Sciences, Biological Sciences, and the Health Sciences. Physical Sciences and Mathematics includes Chemistry; Astronomy and Physics; Earth, Atmospheric, and Ocean Sciences; and Mathematics and Computer Sciences

TABLE B-2: Number and Percentage of Postdoctoral Appointments
Across Employment Sectors, 1981-1997

	1981	1985	1989	1993	1997
Academic	8,628	8,848	11,761	13,264	19,358
Percent	*91.4%*	*87.6%*	*89.4%*	*80.0%*	*80.3%*
Industrial	221	479	555	989	1,663
Percent	*2.3%*	*4.7%*	*4.2%*	*6.0%*	*6.9%*
Government	593	772	835	2,325	3,090
Percent	*6.3%*	*7.6%*	*6.3%*	*14.0%*	*12.8%*
Total	9,442	10,099	13,151	16,578	24,111

Source: 1981, 1985, 1989, 1993, and 1997 Survey of Doctorate Recipients

TABLE B-3: US Citizen and Permanent Resident Postdoctoral Appointees
at US Universities, 1988-1998

	1988	1990	1992	1994	1996	1998
Agricultural Sciences	312	322	353	353	342	347
Biological Sciences	6,110	6,388	6,594	7,283	7,499	7,527
Chemistry	1,331	1,327	1,248	1,427	1,385	1,406
Earth, Atmospheric, and Ocean Sciences	307	377	415	514	504	527
Engineering	587	608	762	1,014	1,050	935
Medical Sciences	3,969	4,440	4,611	5,499	5,475	6,787
Mathematical Sciences	208	139	190	227	258	309
Physics and Astronomy	903	863	976	972	1,065	945
Psychology	425	381	401	426	483	482
Social Sciences	242	247	226	249	308	260
Total US Citizen and Perms	14,420	15,115	15,800	17,986	18,412	19,543

Source: 1988, 1990, 1992, 1994, 1996, and 1998 Survey of Graduate Students and Postdoctorates in
Science and Engineering

TABLE B-4: Percentage of US Citizens and Permanent Residents with Postdoctoral Appointments in US Institutions by Field, 1988-1998

	1988	1990	1992	1994	1996	1998
Agricultural Sciences	67.2%	61.5%	56.0%	50.1%	50.5%	52.1%
Biological Sciences	57.2%	53.5%	50.0%	50.4%	50.2%	48.6%
Chemistry	38.7%	36.4%	34.8%	38.3%	38.7%	37.8%
Earth, Atmospheric, and						
Ocean Sciences	61.9%	63.5%	60.0%	62.4%	58.5%	58.8%
Engineering	34.8%	31.3%	32.3%	39.0%	39.3%	33.0%
Medical Sciences	62.1%	57.3%	52.1%	52.1%	52.1%	55.9%
Mathematical Sciences	54.7%	43.4%	54.9%	53.5%	44.8%	48.1%
Physics and Astronomy	52.1%	45.0%	45.0%	46.0%	49.1%	42.6%
Psychology	85.3%	82.1%	76.4%	77.3%	81.3%	78.8%
Social Sciences	75.6%	56.4%	62.6%	63.8%	69.4%	67.9%
Total	55.2%	51.1%	48.2%	49.4%	49.6%	49.3%

Source: 1988, 1990, 1992, 1994, 1996, and 1998 Survey of Graduate Students and Postdoctorates in Science and Engineering

TABLE B-5: Reasons for Taking First Postdoctoral Appointment, by Field of Doctorate, 1997

	Expected or Additional Training	Work with Specific Person	Training Outside PhD Field	Other Employment Not Available	Other	Total
Biological Sciences	6,404	2,427	1,950	1,779	602	13,162
Percent	*57.2%*	*51.8%*	*57.3%*	*40.4%*	*31.5%*	*54.3%*
Chemistry	865	308	292	551	168	2,184
Percent	*7.7%*	*6.6%*	*8.6%*	*12.5%*	*8.8%*	*9.0%*
Earth, Atmospheric, and						
Ocean Sciences	343	75	75	238	80	811
Percent	*3.1%*	*1.6%*	*2.2%*	*5.4%*	*4.2%*	*3.3%*
Engineering	586	464	288	517	401	2,256
Percent	*5.2%*	*9.9%*	*8.5%*	*11.7%*	*21.0%*	*9.3%*
Medical Sciences	205	137	82	68	74	566
Percent	*1.8%*	*2.9%*	*2.4%*	*1.5%*	*3.9%*	*2.3%*
Physics and Astronomy	1,010	347	175	399	162	2,093
Percent	*9.0%*	*7.4%*	*5.1%*	*9.1%*	*8.5%*	*8.6%*
Social and Behavioral						
Sciences	1,368	564	412	514	305	3,163
Percent	*12.2%*	*12.0%*	*12.1%*	*11.7%*	*15.9%*	*13.1%*
All Postdoctorates	11,197	4,687	3,403	4,406	1,914	24,235
Percent	*100%*	*100%*	*100%*	*100%*	*100%*	*100%*

Source: Survey of Doctorate Recipients, 1997

TABLE B-6: 1997 Status of 1995 Postdoctorates, by Selected Science & Engineering Field

1997 Employment Status	Biological Sciences	Chemistry	Engineering	Physics and Astronomy	Psychology	Total
Postdoc Appointment	3,445	317	281	504	170	5,281
Percent	50.5%	23.2%	27.8%	33.2%	25.3%	38.0%
4 Yr. or Univ. and TenureTrack	899	230	129	253	94	2,288
Percent	13.2%	16.8%	12.7%	16.7%	14.0%	16.5%
Other Academic	1,213	279	103	250	209	2,548
Percent	17.8%	20.4%	10.2%	16.5%	31.1%	18.4%
Industry or Self-Employed	735	342	373	320	73	2,173
Percent	10.8%	25.0%	36.9%	21.1%	10.9%	15.6%
Non-Profit or Government	451	104	102	190	126	1,382
Percent	6.6%	7.6%	10.1%	12.5%	18.8%	10.0%
Unemployed	75	97	24	NA	NA	213
Percent	1.1%	7.1%	2.4%	NA	NA	1.5%
Total 1995 Postdoctoral Appointees	6,818	1,369	1,012	1,517	672	13,885

Source: Merged 1995 and 1997 data from the Survey of Doctorate Recipients

Note:NA = insufficient data to provide reliable information.

TABLE B-7: Sources of Job Advice for Individuals with and without Postdoctoral Appointments

	Best Sources		Utilized Sources	
	Biochemistry Postdoctoral Appointees	Mathematics Postdoctoral Appointees	Biochemistry Postdoctoral Appointees	Mathematics Postdoctoral Appointees
Postdoctoral Mentor	41%	16%	59%	31%
Job Notice in Professional Journal	38%	31%	57%	51%
PhD Adviser	25%	39%	42%	60%
Sent Unsolicited	7%	13%	21%	37%
Other Faculty	16%	27%	39%	56%
Former Professional Contacts	16%	28%	25%	40%
Job Ads On-Campus	3%	6%	13%	13%

Source: *Science* 1999, Vol. 285, p. 1518

TABLE B-8: Comparison of Primary Concerns of Johns Hopkins
University Postdoctoral Appointees in 1992 and 1997

	1992	1997
Future Job Placement	45%	68%
Salary Levels	47%	67%
Dental Insurance	0%	47%
Campus Parking	39%	40%
Research Funding	22%	37%
Personal Safety	60%	31%
Health Insurance	53%	26%
Child Care	29%	26%

Source: *Science* 1999, Vol. 285, pp. 1514 (data collected by Johns Hopkins University Postdoctoral
Association)

TABLE B-9: Median Number of Months Spent in Postdoctoral
Appointment, by Field and Years Since Doctorate

	Years Since Doctorate		
	4 to 6	7 to 10	11 to 20
Agricultural Sciences	20	22	25
Biological Sciences	46	45	38
Chemistry	22	24	22
Earth, Atmospheric, and Ocean Sciences	23	19	16
Physics and Astronomy	34	32	25
Psychology	15	16	20
All Science and Engineering	29	29	26

Source: Survey of Doctorate Recipients, 1995

Notes: Years since doctorate are counted from 1995 when data was collected. Data for the most
current, 1 to 3 years cohort, is not provided since many doctorates are still in postdoctoral positions.

TABLE B-10: Number of Science and Engineering Doctorates by Field, 1975-1998

	1975	1980	1985	1990	1995	1996	1997	1998
Agricultural Sciences	1,067	1,072	1,258	1,321	1,212	1,208	1,112	1,192
Biological Sciences	3,497	3,803	3,793	4,328	5,376	5,723	5,777	5,848
Medical Sciences	462	586	729	956	1,330	1,324	1,422	1,500
Engineering	3,002	2,479	3,166	4,894	6,008	6,305	6,098	5,919
Mathematical Sciences	1,147	962	998	1,597	2,187	2,043	2,030	2,100
Earth, Atmospheric, and Ocean Sciences	634	628	617	769	807	807	897	838
Physics and Astronomy	1,300	983	1,080	1,393	1,652	1,676	1,597	1,584
Chemistry	1,776	1,538	1,836	2,100	2,162	2,148	2,143	2,217
Social Sciences	3,315	2,757	2,647	2,812	3,356	3,474	3,473	3,394
Psychology	2,751	3,098	3,118	3,281	3,279	3,340	3,564	3,681
All Science and Engineering Doctorates	18,951	17,906	19,242	23,451	27,369	28,048	28,113	28,273

Source: Survey of Earned Doctorates, 1920-1998

Note: Includes all doctorates, independent of citizenship status

TABLE B-11: Number of Science and Engineering Doctorates Planning Postdoctoral Study by Field, 1975-1998

	1975	1980	1985	1990	1995	1998
Agricultural Sciences	157	154	238	354	334	327
Biological Sciences	1,923	2,310	2,328	2,827	3,500	3,488
Medical Sciences	58	108	96	160	231	214
Engineering	385	279	425	843	1,193	949
Mathematical Sciences	119	111	147	300	437	367
Earth, Atmospheric, and Ocean Sciences	139	176	213	281	338	306
Physics and Astronomy	611	445	486	765	885	672
Chemistry	811	606	747	927	1,089	943
Social Sciences	139	191	193	225	316	357
Psychology	377	476	485	553	751	882
All Science and Engineering Doctorates	4,719	4,856	5,358	7,235	9,074	8,505

Source: Survey of Earned Doctorates, 1920-1998

TABLE B-12: Source of Support for Academic Postdoctoral Appointees by Field, 1998

	Fellowships	Traineeships	Research Grants	Non-Federal Sources	Total
Agriculture	28	1	345	292	666
Biological Sciences	1,575	1,084	8,557	4,264	15,480
Medical Sciences	1,716	1,548	4,020	4,853	12,137
Engineering	113	21	1,829	867	2,830
Mathematical and Computer Sciences	75	2	370	195	642
Earth, Atmospheric, and Ocean Sciences	71	12	670	144	897
Physics and Astronomy	111	9	1,754	342	2,216
Chemistry	249	28	2,421	1,018	3,716
Social Sciences	35	26	96	226	383
Psychology	79	109	248	176	612
Total	4,052	2,840	20,310	12,377	39,579

Source: Survey of Graduate Students and Postdoctorates in Science and Engineering, 1998

TABLE B-13: Married and Dependent Status of Postdoctoral Appointees in 1997

	HAVE CHILDREN		NO CHILDREN		MARRIED		NOT MARRIED	
	Number	Percent	Number	Percent	Number	Percent	Number	Percent
Agriculture	373	54.7%	309	45.3%	539	79.0%	143	21.0%
Biological Sciences	5,329	40.5%	7,833	59.5%	8,984	68.3%	4,178	31.7%
Medical Sciences	276	48.8%	290	51.2%	345	61.0%	221	39.0%
Engineering	855	37.9%	1,401	62.1%	1,686	74.7%	570	25.3%
Mathematical and Computer Sciences	101	15.3%	557	84.7%	296	45.0%	362	55.0%
Earth, Atmospheric, and Ocean Sciences	345	42.5%	466	57.5%	479	59.1%	332	40.9%
Physics and Astronomy	555	26.5%	1,538	73.5%	1,160	55.4%	933	44.6%
Chemistry	595	27.2%	1,589	72.8%	1,328	60.8%	856	39.2%
Social Sciences	1,118	35.3%	2,045	64.7%	1,931	61.0%	1,232	39.0%
Psychology	856	38.0%	1,398	62.0%	1,425	63.2%	829	36.8%

Source: Survey of Doctorate Recipients, 1997

TABLE B-14: Ratio of the Number of Tenured Faculty to the Number of Doctorates in 1987 and 1997

	Doctorates		Tenured Faculty		Ratio Tenured Faculty/ Doctorates	
	1987	1997	1987	1997	1987	1997
Agriculture	157	281	5,551	6,107	35.4	21.7
Biological Sciences	1,923	3,324	22,967	24,718	11.9	7.4
Medical Sciences	58	197	2,545	3,899	43.9	19.8
Engineering	385	1,000	12,950	15,691	33.6	15.7
Mathematical and Computer Sciences	119	365	9,841	12,554	82.7	34.4
Earth, Atmospheric, and Ocean Sciences	139	309	2,944	3,504	21.2	11.3
Physics and Astronomy	611	654	7,047	7,370	11.5	11.3
Chemistry	811	923	9,334	8,623	11.5	9.3
Social Sciences	516	1,019	24,008	26,137	46.5	25.6
Psychology	377	733	12,404	13,993	32.9	19.1

Source: Survey of Doctorate Recipients, 1987 and 1997

TABLE B-15: Median Postdoctoral Salaries by Employment Sector and Field of Doctorate in 1997 for Doctorate in the Six-Year Cohort, 1991-1996

	Academe	Industry	Government
Life Sciences	$27,000	$33,000	$35,000
Engineering	$30,000	$56,500	$45,000
Physics and Astronomy	$34,000	$48,000	$42,000
Chemistry	$25,000	$40,000	$48,000
Social/Behavioral Sciences	$27,600	$30,000	$35,000

Source: Survey of Doctorate Recipients, 1997

Note: Median salaries are presented only for individuals who received their doctorate between 1991 and 1996 to avoid including senior personnel who might classify a leave position as a postdoctoral appointment. Other fields where not included since the number of data points may be too small to provide accurate information.

TABLE B-16: Median Industrial Salaries in 1997 for Doctorates in the Six-Year PhD Cohort, 1991-1996, by Field and Type of Appointment

	Postdoctoral Positions	Non-Postdoctoral Positions
Life Sciences	33,000	61,000
Engineering	56,500	69,000
Physics and Astronomy	48,000	64,000
Chemistry	40,000	62,400
Social/Behavioral Sciences	30,000	50,000

Note: Median salaries are presented only for individuals who received their doctorate between 1991 and 1996 to avoid including senior personnel who might classify a leave position as a postdoctoral appointment. Other fields where not included since the number of data points may be too small to provide accurate information.

Source: Survey of Doctorate Recipients, 1997

TABLE B-17: Median Government Salaries in 1997 for Doctorates in the Six-Year PhD Cohort, 1991-1996, by Field and Type of Appointment

	Postdoctoral Positions	Non-Postdoctoral Positions
Life Sciences	35,000	50,000
Engineering	45,000	60,000
Physics and Astronomy	42,000	60,000
Chemistry	48,000	60,000
Social/Behavioral Sciences	35,000	51,000

Source: Survey of Doctorate Recipients, 1997

Note: Median salaries are presented only for individuals who received their doctorate between 1991 and 1996 to avoid including senior personnel who might classify a leave position as a postdoctoral appointment. Other fields where not included since the number of data points may be too small to provide accurate information.

TABLE B-18: Number of Postdoctoral Appointments in Selective Survey Years, 1981-1997

	Academic Postdoctoral Positions				
	1981	1985	1989	1993	1997
Life Sciences	5,257	5,294	6,909	7,720	11,253
Engineering	192	187	607	919	1,671
Physics and Astronomy	716	781	1,019	1,635	1,541
Chemistry	1,258	1,235	1,562	1,806	1,621
Social and Behavioral Sciences	894	1,090	1,148	588	2,069

	Industrial Postdoctoral Positions				
	1981	1985	1989	1993	1997
Life Sciences	100	193	217	404	655
Engineering	NA	NA	169	198	140
Physics and Astronomy	55	115	57	79	54
Chemistry	NA	70	NA	240	307
Social and Behavioral Sciences	NA	80	NA	50	465

	Governmental Postdoctoral Positions				
	1981	1985	1989	1993	1997
Life Sciences	332	502	583	1,524	1,594
Engineering	NA	144	NA	144	384
Physics and Astronomy	62	NA	82	150	468
Chemistry	26	59	82	173	217
Social and Behavioral Sciences	88	NA	NA	181	313

Source: 1981, 1985, 1989, 1993, and 1997 Survey of Doctorate Recipients

Note: NA = insufficient data to provide reliable information.

TABLE B-19: Number and Percentage of 1991-1996 Doctorates that Hold Postdoctoral Positions in 1997, by Gender

PhD Field	Male			Female			
	Total Doctorates	Number of Postdocs	Percentage of Male Doctorates in Postdoc Positions	Total Doctorates	Number of Postdocs	Percentage of Female Doctorates in Postdoc Positions	Percentage of all Postdoc Positions Held by Females
Agricultural Sciencs	2,776	219	7.9%	966	133	13.8%	37.8%
Biological Sciences	13,923	5,579	40.1%	9,657	4,011	41.5%	41.8%
Medical Sciences	1,694	122	7.2%	4,035	219	5.4%	64.2%
Engineering	14,683	826	5.6%	2,354	205	8.7%	19.9%
Mathematics	5,327	323	6.1%	1,545	93	6.0%	22.4%
Earth and Atmos Sciences	2,454	479	19.5%	841	144	17.1%	23.1%
Astronomy and Physics	4,957	1,250	25.2%	579	138	23.8%	9.9%
Chemistry	6,453	992	15.4%	2,281	305	13.4%	23.5%
Social Sciences	6,983	312	4.5%	5,284	220	4.2%	41.4%
Psychology	6,604	651	9.9%	11,677	953	8.2%	59.4%
Total	65,854	10,753	16.3%	39,119	6,421	16.4%	37.4%

PhD Field	Male			Female			
	Total Doctorates	Number of Postdocs	Percentage of Male Doctorates in Postdoc Positions	Total Doctorates	Number of Postdocs	Percentage of Female Doctorates in Postdoc Positions	Percentage of all Postdoc Positions Held by Females
Life Sciences	18,393	5,920	32.2%	14,658	4,363	29.8%	42.4%
Engineering	14,683	826	5.6%	2,354	205	8.7%	19.9%
Physical, Math and Comp Sci	19,191	3,044	15.9%	5,246	680	13.0%	18.3%
Social/Behavioral Sci	13,587	963	7.1%	16,861	1,173	7.0%	54.9%
Total	65,854	10,753	16.3%	39,119	6,421	16.4%	37.4%

Source: Survey of Doctorate Recipients, 1997

Appendix C

Results of Survey of Organizations with Postdoctoral Scholars

Little information is available regarding the current status of postdocs as to the compensation, benefits, and services they receive from the institutions in which they serve. Therefore, COSEPUP decided to conduct a very limited survey to gain an understanding of the status quo. By doing so, the committee was able to identify what changes needed to be made in order to enhance the postdoctoral experience.

COSEPUP decided to survey the top 25 academic institutions (in terms of the largest numbers of postdoctoral scholars) and five each of the following: smaller institutions (in terms of number of postdoctoral scholars), medical schools, historically black colleges and universities (HBCUs), industry, research institutions, and government laboratories. The survey was conducted from November 1999 to April 2000.

The survey was conducted of 49 organizations who have postdoctoral scholars. Forty of the 49 organizations responded (82 percent response rate). These organizations are listed below:

Academic Institutions
Arizona State University
Columbia University
Cornell University
Harvard University
Indiana University
Iowa State University
Massachusetts Institute of Technology

Stanford University
Tennessee State University
The University of Michigan
The University of Texas at Austin
University of California, Berkeley
University of California, Los Angeles
University of California, San Diego
University of California, San Francisco
University of Cincinnati
University of Colorado, Boulder
University of Minnesota
University of North Carolina, Chapel Hill
University of Washington
University of Wisconsin, Madison
Virginia Polytechnic Institute and State University
Washington University
Yale University

Medical Schools
John Hopkins University School of Medicine
NYU School of Medicine
University of Medicine and Dentistry of New Jersey
University of Pennsylvania School of Medicine
University of Toronto, Faculty of Medicine
Yeshiva University, Albert Einstein College of Medicine

Government
Los Alamos National Laboratory
Environmental Protection Agency (ORD, NCER, ESRD)
National Oceanic and Atmospheric Administration (NOAA)
US Army Research Laboratory

Industry
Eli Lilly and Company
Microsoft Corporation
Parke-Davis

Research Institutes
Chemical Industry Institute of Toxicology
Fred Hutchinson Cancer Research Center
Rowland Institute for Science

The remainder of this appendix provides the survey questions asked of the institutions with postdoctoral scholars and their responses to those questions.

POSTDOCTORAL SURVEY

Given by the Committee on Science, Engineering, and Public Policy
A Joint Committee of the National Academies

Name:
Organization Name:
Department:
Title:
City:
State, Zip Code:
Daytime Phone:
Email:

Please fill out responses to each question below. If none of the choices are appropriate, please explain your organization's policy or service in the space provided. If you do not have enough information to answer a question, please mark the Do not know option.

___ Please check here if you would like your data to remain confidential.

1. **Does your organization provide job placement services for your postdocs? (Select all that apply.)**
   ___ Services are available from an assigned individual whose sole responsibility is to work with postdocs (and graduate students).
   ___ Services are available on-site as part of general student/employee services.
   ___ Job placement tends to be the responsibility of the adviser.
   ___ Job placement is the responsibility of the postdoc.
   ___ Job placement is a dual responsibility of the adviser and postdoc.
   ___ Do not know.
   ___ Other, please explain:

2. **Does your organization establish minimum and/or maximum stipend levels for postdocs?** If yes, please specify dollar value for minimum and/or maximum stipends. If no, why not?

   ___ Yes   ___ No   ___ Do not know

If yes, please specify dollar values in the space provided.
If no, why not?
Other, please explain:

3. Does your organization provide medical benefits to all postdocs and their dependents? (Select all that apply.)

___ The organization pays for medical benefits for all postdocs and their dependents.
___ The organization provides medical benefits at full compensation to all postdocs but not their dependents.
___ The organization requires that postdoc advisers pay for the medical benefits of their postdocs.
___ The organization informs postdocs of medical benefit plans that they and their dependents can enter at own expense (if at a discounted rate, please provide the percent discounted). Discount %:
___ The source of the postdoc's funding determines medical benefit availability.
___ No medical benefits are provided by the organization.
___ Do not know.
___ Other, please explain:

4. How is the postdoc made aware of benefits that are and are not available? (Select all that apply.)

___ A formal letter of acceptance is sent prior to arrival to each postdoc by the organization and/or postdoc adviser outlining the organization's policies on paid-for benefits.
___ An orientation meeting or equivalent is given to all entering postdocs discussing benefits.
___ It is the responsibility of the adviser to discuss benefit availability with the postdoc.
___ No information is formally provided.
___ Do not know.
___ Other, please explain:

5. Which of the following benefits is provided at full compensation to ALL postdocs, regardless of adviser or funding source? (Select all that apply. If a benefit is offered at a reduced cost to the postdoc, please specify percent discounted.)

Dental insurance	Discount %:
Disability	Discount %:
Maternity/paternity leave	
Email/computer accounts	
Campus housing	Discount %:
Cost of living salary adjustments	
Merit increases	
Child daycare	Discount %:
Vacation time	
Sick leave	
Library	Discount %:
On-campus parking (or equivalent)	Discount %:
Retirement (401K, 403B or equivalent)	Discount %:
Life insurance	Discount %:
Travel expenses to conferences when the postdoc is presenting	Discount %:
Travel expenses to conferences when the postdoc is not presenting	Discount %:
Do not know	
Other benefits, please specify:	
A.	A. Other Discount %:
B.	B. Other Discount %:
C.	C. Other Discount %:

6. **Does the organization have staff that deals specifically with the special needs of non-US or foreign national postdocs?**

___ Yes
___ No
___ No, handled by postdoc adviser
___ Do not know
___ Other, please explain:

7. **If offered, in what areas do foreign national postdocs receive assistance?**
   (Select all that apply.)

___ Visas
___ Housing
___ Tax advice

___ Credit references
___ Social Security
___ Drivers License
___ English language or writing classes
___ No special services are available
___ Do not know
___ Other, please explain:

8. Does the organization require performance evaluations throughout a postdoc's appointment?

___ Regular performance evaluations are required.
___ Each postdoc is evaluated by an appointed advisory committee that includes individuals beyond their direct advisers.
___ Documented progress reviews are performed by the respective adviser at his/her discretion.
___ No official performance reviews of any type are required.
___ Do not know.
___ Other, please explain:

9. How is the duration of a postdoctoral appointment determined? (Select all that apply.)

___ Determined prior to postdoc's arrival.
___ Determined by an appointed advisory committee after a formal presentation.
___ Determined primarily by the adviser at any time point throughout a postdoc's appointment.
___ Determined primarily by source of funding and/or funding availability.
___ Do not know.
___ Other mechanism, please explain:

10. Is there a Postdoctoral Association or equivalent on-site?

___ A Postdoctoral Association or equivalent is available and run by postdocs themselves.
___ A Postdoctoral Association or equivalent is available and run by the institution.
___ An Association that serves both doctoral students and postdocs is available.
___ No organizations are available for postdocs. [Go to question 12]
___ Do not know. [Go to question 12]
___ Other, please explain:

11. If your organization has a Postdoctoral Association or equivalent, what are its main functions? (Select all that apply.)

___ A conduit for information services such as housing, childcare, visas for international postdocs, and general personal living questions.

___ Acts as a liaison between postdoc and the administration.

___ Provides appointed representatives to the organization's administrative councils.

___ Provides professional and social activities for postdocs.

___ Do not know.

___ Other, please explain:

12. Who are the neutral parties responsible at the organization for handling grievances of the postdoc? (Select all that apply.)

___ Human Resource staff person

___ An ombudsperson

___ A dean or department chairperson

___ The adviser

___ Do not know

___ Other, please explain:

13. How are postdocs classified at your organizations? (Select all that apply. For multiple answers, please define the nature of the each appointment classification.)

Faculty   Description:
Student   Description:
Staff   Description:
Employee   Description:
Fellow   Description:
Associate   Description:
Trainee   Description:
Other, please specify: Description:

14. Please indicate how many postdocs are currently serving appointments at this organization? (Please provide the most current information available.)

___ Less than 50

___ 50 to 100

___ 101 to 250
___ 251 to 500
___ 501 to 750
___ 751 to 1000
___ More than 1000
___ Do not know

Data from 10

Thank you for taking the time to complete this survey.

Survey Results

1. Does your organization provide job placement services for your post-docs? (Select all that apply.).

| | Responses | |
	Number	Percent
Services are available from an assigned individual whose sole responsibility is to work with postdocs (and graduate students).	7	17.5%
Services are available on-site as part of general student/employee services.	13	32.5%
Job placement tends to be the responsibility of the adviser.	4	10.0%
Job placement is the responsibility of the postdoc.	12	30.0%
Job placement is a dual responsibility of the adviser and postdoc.	28	70.0%
Do not know	0	0.0%
Other	9	22.5%
Non-Respondents	0	

The "other" responses were consistent with the primary responses, which indicate only moderate job placement activity for postdocs on the part of institutions. A few mentioned such resources as career centers, job fairs, job placement web sites, and general student services, and several reported that job placement activities are localized and vary by institutional unit.

2. Does your organization establish minimum and/or maximum stipend levels for postdocs? If yes, please specify dollar value for minimum and/or maximum stipends. If no, why not?

Yes   55% (22 responses)   No   45% (18 responses)

For "yes" responses, the values followed a consistent pattern, which varied by sector. Among universities, minimum levels tended to follow the NIH scale (which begins with a stipend of $26,256); a few were lower. Among the national laboratories and other facilities, most salaries began in the $40,000 to $50,000 range, with lows in the 30s. Maximum government stipends were in the 50s, with a high of $64,750. Some national labs offered "add-on" amounts for "critical skills," from $2,000-$10,000. In industry, stipends beginning in the 30s were common.

For "no" responses, institutions enumerated a range of ambiguities that inhibited the establishment of uniform stipend levels, including the wide variety of job titles and policy differences among departments, schools, or laboratories. Several institutions reported that policies were being prepared.

Some institutions reported the use of other, more subjective criteria to set stipend levels, including the "experience/potential of the postdoc" and the "norms of the field."

Many institutions noted that salary levels for postdocs on fellowships or other outside support are not set by the institution.

3. Does your organization provide medical benefits to all postdocs and their dependents? (Select all that apply.)

Academic Institutions (N = 30)

	Responses	
	Number	Percent
The organization pays for medical benefits for all postdocs and their dependents.	3	10.0%
The organization provides medical benefits at full compensation to all postdocs but not their dependents.	3	10.0%

The organization requires that postdoc advisers pay for the medical benefits of their postdocs.	5	16.7%
The organization informs postdocs of medical benefit plans that they and their dependents can enter at own expense. Percent discounted: Group Rate Plan. (one response at 80%)	7	23.3%
The source of the postdoc's funding determines medical benefit availability.	11	36.7%
No medical benefits are provided by the organization.	2	6.7%
Do not know	0	0.0%
Other medical benefits	14	46.7%
Non-Respondents	0	

Non-Academic Organizations (N = 10)

	Responses	
	Number	Percent
The organization pays for medical benefits for all postdocs and their dependents.	5	55.6%
The organization provides medical benefits at full compensation to all postdocs but not their dependents.	1	11.1%
The organization requires that postdoc advisers pay for the medical benefits of their postdocs.	0	0.0%
The organization informs postdocs of medical benefit plans that they and their dependents can enter at own expense. Percent discounted: Group Rate Plan. (one response at 80%)	1	11.1%
The source of the postdoc's funding determines medical benefit availability.	0	0.0%
No medical benefits are provided by the organization.	0	0.0%
Do not know	0	0.0%

Other medical benefits	2	22.2%

Non-Respondents	1

Among universities, many reported that they provided medical coverage only for those postdocs considered employees; i.e., those paid from research grants ("equivalent to other research faculty/staff").

By contrast, postdocs on fellowships or other external funding support (which includes many foreign postdocs) were less certain of support. Some could count on coverage from their own grant (e.g., the NRC Associateship provided full coverage); others could not, and had to arrange for coverage on their own ("full-time postdocs required to have benefits by state law, except NIH, who don't qualify"). Some universities allowed these externally funded postdocs to buy into available group plans.

Some universities required coverage for all postdocs, regardless of funding source. This meant that those postdocs not paid by the university or covered independently had to be picked up by the adviser or department ("must be paid by employing department").

Postdocs whose coverage was provided by universities received only individual plans. Coverage for spouses and dependents was expected to be paid for by the postdoc.

Typically, industry and government labs offered postdocs the same medical plans offered to employees, with the majority of the premium paid by the employer.

4.   How is the postdoc made aware of benefits that are and are not available? (Select all that apply.)

Academic Institutions (N = 30)

	Responses	
	Number	Percent
A formal letter of acceptance is sent prior to arrival to each postdoc by the organization and/or postdoc adviser outlining the organization's policies on paid-for benefits.	10	33.3%
An orientation meeting or equivalent is given to all entering postdocs discussing benefits.	10	33.3%

It is the responsibility of the adviser to discuss benefit availability with the postdoc.	14	46.7%
No information is formally provided.	3	7.5%
Do not know	0	0.0%
Other	13	43.3%
Non-Respondents	0	

Non-Academic Organizations (N = 10)

	Responses	
	Number	Percent
A formal letter of acceptance is sent prior to arrival to each postdoc by the organization and/or postdoc adviser outlining the organization's policies on paid-for benefits.	6	60.0%
An orientation meeting or equivalent is given to all entering postdocs discussing benefits.	7	70.0%
It is the responsibility of the adviser to discuss benefit availability with the postdoc.	2	20.0%
No information is formally provided.	3	7.5%
Do not know	0	0.0%
Other	3	30.0%
Non-Respondents	0	

The "other" responses indicate that some institutions do not have a central-ized mechanism by which to communicate with postdocs about benefits and other institutional matters. Universities described a number of avenues by which postdocs may or may not receive information ("generally receive information from department administrators," "most send letters," "responsibility of depart-ment or center, not adviser"). Several had no certain process ("Often business managers take on the responsibility of informing postdocs"). Some were in the process of including benefits information in a formal acceptance letter.

5.   Which of the following benefits is provided at full compensation to ALL postdocs, regardless of adviser or funding source? (Select all that apply. If a benefit is offered at a reduced cost to the postdoc, please specify percent discounted.)

Academic Institutions (N = 30)

	Responses	
	Number	Percent
Dental insurance	8	27.6%
Disability	8	27.6%
Maternity/paternity leave	9	31.0%
Email/computer accounts	26	89.7%
Campus housing	4	13.8%
Cost of living salary adjustments	1	3.4%
Merit increases	7	24.1%
Child daycare	2	6.9%
Vacation time	15	51.7%
Sick leave	13	44.8%
Library	26	89.7%
On-campus parking (or equivalent)	13	44.8%
Retirement (401K, 403B or equivalent)	7	24.1%
Life insurance	9	31.0%
Travel expenses to conferences when the postdoc is presenting	3	10.3%
Travel expenses to conferences when the postdoc is not presenting	2	6.9%
Do not know	1	3.4%
Other benefits	4	13.8%
Non-Respondents	1	

Non-Academic Organizations (N = 10)

	Responses Number	Percent
Dental insurance	8	88.9%
Disability	8	88.9%
Maternity/paternity leave	7	77.8%
Email/computer accounts	8	88.9%
Campus housing	0	0.0%
Cost of living salary adjustments	3	33.3%
Merit increases	4	44.4%
Child daycare	3	33.3%
Vacation time	8	88.9%
Sick leave	8	88.9%
Library	7	77.8%
On-campus parking (or equivalent)	7	77.8%
Retirement (401K, 403B or equivalent)	6	66.7%
Life insurance	8	88.9%
Travel expenses to conferences when the postdoc is presenting	9	100.0%
Travel expenses to conferences when the postdoc is not presenting	8	88.9%
Do not know	1	11.1%
Other benefits	2	22.2%
Non-Respondents	1	

Some common "other" benefits offered to postdocs included access to recreational tickets, athletic facilities, credit unions, student unions, tuition wavers, travel accident insurance, and alumni privileges. Some institutions offered various leave benefits, including one vacation week for marriage, an illness pay program (up to one month), and six weeks of paid parental leave. At many universities, leave policies were determined by the adviser. Several institutions mentioned retirement plans, with most requiring a vesting period of two or more years. Several national labs covered relocation expenses.

6.   Does the organization have staff that deals specifically with the special needs of non-US or foreign national postdocs?

	Responses	
	Number	Percent
Yes	28	70.0%
No	3	7.5%
No, handled by postdoc adviser	3	7.5%
Do not know	0	0.0%
Other, please explain:	6	15.0%
Non-Respondents	0	0

Most of the "other" responses indicated a pattern of offering postdocs the same access to international services as students and other scholars.

7.   If offered, in what areas do foreign national postdocs receive assistance? (Select all that apply.)

	Responses	
	Number	Percent
Visas	36	97.3%
Housing	20	54.1%
Tax advice	23	62.2%
Credit references	4	10.8%

Social Security	16	43.2%
Drivers License	4	10.8%
English language or writing classes	21	56.8%
No special services are available	1	2.7%
Do not know	0	0.0%
Other	7	18.9%
Non-Respondents	3	

Other areas where foreign national postdocs were offered assistance included obtaining a Social Security number, a drivers license, and tax treaty information. Several institutions offered help with household furnishings and support groups for spouses and dependents.

8. Does the organization require performance evaluations throughout a postdoc's appointment?

Academic Institutions (N = 30)

	Responses	
	Number	Percent
Regular performance evaluations are required.	5	16.7%
Each postdoc is evaluated by an appointed advisory committee that includes individuals beyond their direct advisers.	0	0.0%
Documented progress reviews are performed by the respective adviser at his/her discretion.	4	13.3%
No official performance reviews of any type are required.	14	46.7%
Do not know	1	3.3%
Other	6	20.0%
Non-Respondents	0	

Non-Academic Organizations (N = 10)

	Responses	
	Number	Percent
Regular performance evaluations are required.	7	70.0%
Each postdoc is evaluated by an appointed advisory committee that includes individuals beyond their direct advisers.	1	10.0%
Documented progress reviews are performed by the respective adviser at his/her discretion.	1	10.0%
No official performance reviews of any type are required.	1	10.0%
Do not know	0	0.0%
Other	0	0.0%
Non-Respondents	0	

The responses to this question indicated that some institutions are examining and/or revising their policies on evaluations ("may change"; "will be implementing performance management for all postdocs"). Others described optional or discretionary approaches to evaluation ("depends on program"; "depends on funding source"; "varies by unit"). Several institutions expected the adviser to take responsibility for evaluations, without formal reporting to the institution.

9. How is the duration of a postdoctoral appointment determined? (Select all that apply.)

	Responses	
	Number	Percent
Determined prior to postdoc's arrival.	18	45.0%
Determined by an appointed advisory committee after a formal presentation.	1	2.5%
Determined primarily by the adviser at any time point throughout a postdoc's appointment.	23	57.5%

Determined primarily by source of funding and/or funding availability.	22	55.0%
Do not know	0	0.0%
Other mechanism	13	32.5%
Non-Respondents	0	

Many institutions said that they had firm limits to postdoctoral terms (typically three, four, or five years). Others allowed for extensions "in special cases," which sometimes required the specific approval of an administration officer. Other policies were to appoint postdocs for a year at a time, with renewal depending on funding and performance, or to allow the length of training to vary by field and source of funding, with no suggested limit.

10. Is there a Postdoctoral Association or equivalent on-site?

	Responses	
	Number	Percent
A Postdoctoral Association or equivalent is available and run by postdocs themselves.	11	27.5%
A Postdoctoral Association or equivalent is available and run by the institution.	1	2.5%
An Association that serves both doctoral students and postdocs is available.	0	0.0%
No organizations are available for postdocs.	23	57.5%
Do not know	1	2.5%
Other	4	10.0%
Non-Respondents	0	

The "other" responses mentioned one other postdoctoral association run by postdocs, a "postdoctoral council." One institution reported an association run jointly by postdocs and the institution. Most indicated that postdoctoral activities were either informal or confined to the lab, department, or a particular group (e.g., Chinese Students and Scholars).

11. If your organization has a Postdoctoral Association or equivalent, what are its main functions? (Select all that apply.)

	Responses	
	Number	Percent
A conduit for information services such as housing, child care, visas for international postdocs, and general personal living questions.	7	50.0%
Acts as a liaison between postdoc and the administration.	11	78.6%
Provides appointed representatives to the organization's administrative councils.	5	35.7%
Provides professional and social activities for postdocs.	13	92.9%
Do not know	1	7.1%
Other	1	7.1%
Non-Respondents (based on 16 responses to Question 10)	2	

One organization reported that its office of postdoctoral programs worked closely with the postdoctoral council (run by postdocs). For example, the office and council "...co-sponsor responsible conduct in research training, career workshops, a career fair, and survival skills training. [The office] is establishing mentor guidelines. It enforces the University policy on postdoctoral appointments which sets minimum stipends and benefits...."

12. Who are the neutral parties responsible at the organization for handling grievances of the postdoc? (Select all that apply.)

	Responses	
	Number	Percent
Human Resources staff person	19	51.4%
An ombudsperson	16	43.2%

A dean or department chairperson	28	75.7%
The adviser	17	45.9%
Do not know	1	2.7%
Other	12	32.4%

Non-Respondents

Institutions reported a wide range of "other" methods for handling postdoc grievances, from "same as junior faculty" to "office of grad studies and research" and "ombudsfolks—faculty peer adviser selected by postdocs"). A few placed most of the responsibility on a single person ("vice provost for research," "provost," "always dean or chair; sometimes human resources, too"), while a smaller number described a more flexible process ("dispute resolution guideline for College of Medicine postdoctoral fellows; ad hoc committee makes recommendation to associate dean for research and graduate education"). At an industry lab, a variety of avenues were available, including human resources, a Scientific Advisory Committee of senior scientists, and "line management." National labs mentioned both laboratory or division managers and a postdoctoral committee.

13. **How are postdocs classified at your organizations?** (Select all that apply. For multiple answers, please define the nature of the each appointment classification.)

	Responses	
	Number	Percent
Faculty	5	12.5%
Student	5	12.5%
Staff	4	10.0%
Employee	16	40.0%
Fellow	20	50.0%
Associate	9	22.5%
Trainee	14	35.0%

Other please specify	9	22.5%

Non-Respondents	0

The "other" ways to classify postdocs varied widely, including "employees-in-training," "scholars," "visiting postdoctoral scholars," and "students in training." One national lab used three categories of fellow, depending on funding source. Many titles were variations on the two commonest classifications—"fellow" and "research associate"—but a few seemed to indicate a desire for a more functional definition: "guest researcher," "academic professional," "trainees—irrespective of funding source," and "someone receiving further training in the laboratory."

14. Please indicate how many postdocs are currently serving appointments at this organization? (Please provide the most current information available.)

	Responses	
	Number	Percent
Less than 50	6	15.4%
50 to 100	7	17.9%
101 to 250	8	20.5%
251 to 500	3	7.7%
501 to 750	2	5.1%
751 to 1000	6	15.4%
More than 1000	7	17.9%
Do not know	0	0.0%
Non-respondents	1	

Appendix D

Summary of Workshop on Enhancing the Postdoctoral Experience

DECEMBER 21, 1999
WASHINGTON, DC

SUMMARY

An all-day workshop on the postdoctoral experience was attended by an over flow group of more than 100 people from universities, national labs, federal agencies, research institutes, industries, foundations, and disciplinary societies, including 25 who were invited to make brief presentations. The committee was impressed by the high level of interest in this topic, and by the spirited opinions of all participants, including postdocs, researchers, administrators, and other concerned parties. (A list of workshop participants follows this summary.)

The discussions, chaired by COSEPUP member Mildred Dresselhaus (and attended by COSEPUP Chair Maxine Singer for part of the session), were organized by the following topics: administrative status, compensation and benefits, classification and titles, career planning, postdoctoral offices and associations, foreign-national postdocs, and good mentoring practices.

The comments were too extensive and diverse to capture in a single brief document. This summation, therefore, is intended to offer a representative and informal sampling of specific comments from a diverse group of people and institutions. Many of the comments reflect efforts to enhance the postdoctoral experience by improving the status, working conditions, and recognition of postdocs.

ADMINISTRATIVE STRUCTURES

- Institutional goals for postdocs vary widely by field and sector. For example, preparing a postdoc for "independence" does not fit the industrial culture, where more research is done in teams.
- Postdocs [at universities] may be "shadow people." They don't have a place. Sometimes we have to use certain titles to get what we want for them.
- At Mayo, we classify them as research fellow (1-3 years), then senior research fellow (4-7 years), then research associate, which can last indefinitely.
- At Albert Einstein College of Medicine, a postdoctoral office was created four years ago to handle postdoc appointments, benefits, housing, etc. The office sends a letter to advisers after 18-24 months informing them how long a postdoc has been in their lab and whether it's time for a salary increase as required by guidelines. In the fourth year an extensive letter is sent asking for a CV and publication record; the PI and department chair evaluate the next step: will the postdoc be renewed for a fifth (and final) year? After that they either leave or become a research associate, with faculty benefits. This keeps them from falling through the cracks.
- Each institution needs to rewrite policy to suit its particular mission and pass it around to postdocs and faculty.
- The University of Pennsylvania started a postdoc policy in 1996 for the medical school.
- A postdoctoral office must not infringe on the postdoc-adviser relationship.
- At Caltech, they're between faculty and staff and students. When we started the postdoctoral scholar position, they wanted oversight because they wanted a relationship with the administration, not just the faculty.
- At NIST we have central funding, like portable fellowships, so the postdoc doesn't have to be stuck with one adviser. In several cases we've switched them to new advisers.
- UPenn keeps a database on all postdocs, including place and date of terminal degree, visa status, research field, what they've published.
- At Alabama/Birmingham all phases of postdoctoral appointments had been left to the discretion of each department. One of the first priorities of the postdoctoral office was to identify all postdocs on campus and create a database. The disparity between what postdocs were being paid became disturbingly evident, and steps are now being taken to bring salaries more in line with national standards.
- When a Howard Hughes grant is initiated, we have a contract with terms and conditions. It's still hard for us to track how fellows are treated. We

stipulate that $5,000 of the institution's allowance is for health benefits, but we see that some postdocs are getting it and some not.

- At Chicago we'd like more open and fair hiring, through a central source. It's difficult, because now it's done when you meet someone at a congress and talk them into writing you into their next grant.
- At Vanderbilt we require annual reappointment and ask department chairs to approve it. This allows institutional controls. I refuse to reappoint without suitable salary level, justification, and an evaluation
- At Cincinnati, we approved a postdoc policy two weeks ago. We've been working on it for two years: health, vacation, maternity leave, drugs, salary at NRSA levels, and benefits from general university funds.
- The University of California did a broad "vision statement" for postdocs in 1998, and each of the nine campuses is trying to conform.
- At UCLA, with 900 postdocs, the graduate division (not the university) took the initiative to put them in the same division, with the same facilities and benefits.

CAREER PLANNING AND TRANSITIONS

- Postdocs need skills that are applicable in any career. A postdoc must gain experience for the next career step. They're not just a person in your lab.
- Most advisers are academics; they don't know what industry expects. They need to hear more from the "final" employers.
- We shouldn't use the term "alternative careers." This implies that anything outside the university is inferior: public policy, writing, teaching. These are just "careers."
- Industry employers are looking for "soft" skills—those not developed at the bench.
- The Burroughs Wellcome Fund provides "bridging awards" of 40-45K for the transitional time after a postdoc.
- A transitional grant isn't needed. It may take a year or so for a postdoc to get up to speed, especially if changing fields; after that you can begin to see how they'll do. They should start looking for a job after three years, and five years is a reasonable time to figure out if this work is for you.
- Five years is plenty to see if a person is going to be an individual investigator; you may know even when they get their PhD. The difficulty is, if they don't seem ready there aren't a lot of other options.
- At UPenn, the time limit is five years; after that they go either to 1) staff scientist or 2) academic track, where they start getting independent funding. The most rapidly growing sector in science is the soft-money positions, like post-postdoc.

- At Hopkins, the limit for postdocs is six years, but you can come in after working somewhere else. We need an overall time limit.
- Both UCSF and the University of Chicago sponsor science career forum at which postdocs can give poster presentations and meet with employers.
- At Alabama/Birmingham, each postdoc can take at least one class per year, paid for by the postdoctoral office. We help those who want experience teaching and compensate for their time away from the lab.
- At Einstein, there is no formal career planning office, but monthly workshops about 1) academic careers, led by new assistant professors who had postdocs, and 2) other careers, with people from scientific publishing, patent law, journals, and Wall Street.
- Postdocs need to know how to teach. Being "allowed" to teach is the wrong word!
- Teaching is very time-consuming if done well. It has to be worked out with the adviser.
- Some institutions don't hold to NIH standards. Postdocs are in a very vulnerable situation. If more had portable grants and could move, they'd be in a stronger position to enhance their career.
- NIH has five-week courses three times a year in writing, speaking, etc. Some fellows have adjunct jobs teaching in the evening.
- Every postdoc should attend at least one professional meeting a year.
- Women are still at a disadvantage in science. A disproportionate number go into soft-money positions. According to a William and Mary survey, dissatisfaction is higher among women than among men. Women shouldn't be penalized for taking time to start a family.

CLASSIFICATION AND TITLES

- NSF grantees are getting older, over 30; a lot are married, a third have significant debt. They need benefits.
- Nobody's categories are perfect; each institution has to adapt something that works. Postdocs should get the best of both worlds, not the worst of both worlds.
- Some of the most gifted postdocs may be penalized if they're classified as fellows; the institution may or may not come up with health benefits.
- At UPenn we consider postdocs in advanced research training, in preparation for next career steps, whatever they might be. We have an obligation to train them. From that definition comes everything else. But we have two classes of people doing the same thing and treated differently by federal regulations. We have federally funded NRSA postdocs, on training grants, then we have the large majority supported by RO1s, which OMB Circular A21 calls a fee for service situation, who are taxed like employees and get benefits.

- At Eli Lilly Co, there are 75 postdocs who are classified as "postdoctoral scientist/fixed-duration employees." Ten years ago all employees were considered full-time; now there are many contractors.
- At West Virginia, a postdoc is on a research track that can go on forever, but it affords a way to do that with benefits.
- At the University of Medicine and Dentistry of New Jersey, we define them as students in training. Health is picked up by the grant, or if not, by the PI. It's university policy. We supplement grants if they're too low from the university foundation. After four years they become employees and get institutional benefits. Monitoring doesn't work at the local level.
- OMB A21 has created some problems and affected the rate of compensation. There are efforts to change that.

COMPENSATION AND BENEFITS

- Postdocs are not trainees; they're producing most of the results in the labs of America. We owe it to ourselves to compensate them right from the start. It would be better to have a smaller number of postdocs but better paid. They might be expected to do more. Now, it's 'My postdoc doesn't work hard, but what do you expect for 25K?"
- Postdocs with a MD degree are paid on the house officer salary scale, which irritates PhDs. But if you brought them down to PhD scale, you wouldn't get any MD's to do research.
- At Caltech if the amount of stipend doesn't meet our minimum, we insist that the PI bring them up to that.
- We have an ombudsperson at NIH and it is fabulously useful, especially when you don't have someone in the lab to talk to.
- NIH raised the [NRSA] stipend because they had a lot of money in FY99. It was based on a general feeling that the scale was low, not on a philosophical change. If this report recommends a raise, it doesn't mean it will be done, but it will provide a general tone.
- At UC, a postdoc receives full benefits: health, dental, parental leave. No retirement. Five years is the legal limit of how long you can keep someone without paying into retirement.
- At Einstein, 85 percent of postdocs are on the NIH grants of PIs. The lab is required to pick up any difference below NRSA.
- At Vanderbilt, trainees and research grant people get paid the same. The trainees don't get retirement, but they also don't pay FICA, so they come out essentially the same.
- The issue about pay is one of basic fairness. We're losing the best and brightest people. We've got to get the salaries up, like at Los Alamos, where we pay 45K. They're 8-10 years behind when they start working

[in permanent positions]. These people are the software that drives science.

- At UC, there is no money from the regents or legislature. We need that. We need to speak out, justify it. Postdocs need reasonable compensation.
- We make them work like dogs and then cast them off at the end.
- If you give them 40K, they'll have to take a salary cut to get a job.
- We're losing American researchers. To someone from another country, 26K and get in the door, that's huge.
- At Howard Hughes we try to be flexible with allowances. If a fellow has a spouse with benefits, we let the fellow use that for child care.
- At JPL and Caltech salary is 42K, except slightly higher for computer science and electrical engineering. The lab picks up about 70 percent of benefits. There are 30 days vacation.
- At Iowa, salaries are now set at twice the graduate stipend; mid-upper 30s. full benefits, except retirement.
- At NIST, they try to match the salary of the average land-grant university assistant professor at approximately 50K, plus $5,500 for travel.
- NRSAs are considered stipends, not salaries, to offset the cost of living during training. The philosophy behind them is to share costs among postdoc, adviser/institution, and NIH.
- Vacations are often a difficult issue, since advisers are reluctant to delay the lab work. If a postdoc is funded on an RO1 through the payroll system, the benefits are the same as for other employees; for fellows there is seldom any provision for vacation.
- Full-time employee benefits have a cost; at UPenn the overhead rate is 31 percent.

EVALUATIONS

- There should be an annual appraisal of both the adviser and the postdoc. These should go to the director of the institution and be part of the basis for discussion of their performance.
- The institution has a responsibility to report back to the sponsors. It's usually public money. This is viewed as onerous, but I've also heard complaints from PIs that private institutions ask for even more information.
- Lilly is just starting evaluations for postdocs. They write up objectives at beginning of year. There's a mid-term review, and at the end they look back at how they've progressed.
- From a practical standpoint, postdocs may never get written evaluations, but maybe the guide will help get more consulting and evaluating on an informal basis.
- At UT/Memphis, fellows and residents are reviewed by various committees once a month, and again every six months. It's very specific.

FOREIGN POSTDOCS

- According to NSF data, about half of the postdocs come from abroad, and about 50 percent of those stay on in the US. This varies by field as well. Returning home is a function of the educational system and job prospects in the country.
- According to an AAMC study, in the last five years many more foreign postdocs, especially Chinese, have stayed, as have Eastern Europeans. Western Europeans do not stay.
- In the early 1990s, more Chinese students stayed in the United States because of the 1992 Chinese Student Protection Act passed by Congress in response to the Tienimen Square Protest. The Act allowed students from the People's Republic of China to apply for permanent residency in 1993. The Act has expired and it is now difficult for students on temporary visas to convert to permanent residency status.
- Scientists should not be isolated. Science is increasingly international. In the US there is little recognition of the value of going abroad, even though NSF offers grants for this.
- There are cases where Asian postdocs are treated as cheap labor and paid the minimum allowed by the immigration office (14K).

MENTORING

- Advisers may experience conflicts between their own best interests and the postdoc's. The postdoc is in some ways at the mercy of the adviser in making choices.
- Postdocs need to lay out a roadmap of expectations and goals.
- Postdocs must develop skills they'll need for the future. They need to spell this out in advance in a letter. That's difficult when on PI grant, because the PI doesn't want to let the postdoc out of the lab. It has to be spelled out.
- At Lilly, adviser selection is done with care. They have to demonstrate they've been successful in mentoring technicians before they can get a postdoc. Postdocs meet with a science council of senior management to showcase their work, network, and discuss any issue or grievance.
- You need oversight of mentoring by senior colleagues or postdoc committee meetings: the fellow, the adviser, and someone else. We need written evaluations; in industry you'd never think of not having them. There's a huge imbalance of power. I take a risk in coming here today.
- At NIH we encourage multiple mentors. We don't have mentoring committees. This seems like a good idea, but faculty members don't like it, and fellows thought it might be confusing having more than one adviser.

A formal system where someone is criticizing the adviser has problems, but feedback is important.

- At Pitt we require formation of a postdoc mentoring committee. Postdocs pick potential role models. Nothing contentious happens, but in rare cases where there are problems [with the adviser], this can pick it up. In most cases the postdocs get valuable feedback on their work.
- At Einstein, we have weekly work-in-progress sessions. All postdocs present their work once a year. If a person is floundering, the group will get together specially and advise.
- At MIT, when postdocs are going to give papers, they give a dry run for us first.
- Graduate students need mentoring before they begin a postdoc on what to expect and what questions to ask.

POSTDOCTORAL ASSOCIATIONS (PDAS)

- PDAs are essential so postdocs are not marginalized.
- At Einstein a committee of 3-4 postdocs runs an association which deals with intellectual issues, social issues, housing; holds postdoc programs 4-5 times per year for faculty and postdocs.
- At Mayo, a PDA reduces the isolation. There are labs right next door you never know about. It expands the vision of what we can do with science. Now I'm doing something different from what I thought I wanted to do.
- At NIEHS faculty resisted us in the beginning because they thought we were trying to unionize. That isn't true any more. We have many programs. It is important to my professional development.
- Howard Hughes fellows meet once a year and postdocs present their research and network.
- At Johns Hopkins, the PDA provides a liaison with the administration, creates a social network, reduces the isolation. When we bring things to the administration they are more than willing to help us. For example, in the last few months we've arranged dental insurance. Each department pays $8 per postdoc per year to support the organization.
- We started out feeling that we didn't have a voice. We got officers, and now have good communication with the administration. It should be run by postdocs; the administration won't know to come up with these issues.

GENERAL POINTS

- Funding agencies have a responsibility to set guidelines that promote best practices.
- The guide should have more "how-to" information: what should the post-

doc be asking of the university and adviser? What should the mentor ask of the postdoc?
- We don't want to be heavy-handed, but the time is right to raise the bar for both postdocs and advisers. Both can do better.

PARTICIPANTS LIST

Workshop on Enhancing the Postdoctoral Experience
December 21, 1999

The National Academies
Washington, DC

COSEPUP Members

Mildred S. Dresselhaus
Chair, COSEPUP Postdoc Guidance
    Group *and*
Institute Professor of Electrical
    Engineering and Physics
Massachusetts Institute of Technology

Maxine F. Singer
Chair, COSEPUP *and*
President, Carnegie Institution of
    Washington

Workshop Participants

Clifford Attkisson
Dean of Graduate Studies
Associate Vice Chancellor of
    Student Academic Affairs
University of California, San Francisco
San Francisco, California

Jack Bennink
Chief, Viral Immunology Section
NIAID, National Institutes of Health
Bethesda, Maryland

Etty Benveniste
Associate Dean, Office of Postdoc
    Education
University of Alabama, Birmingham
Birmingham, Alabama

Beverly Berger
Director, Office of University
    Partnerships
Department of Energy
Washington, DC

Sandra Blackwood
Program Coordinator
Office of Postdoc Education
University of Alabama, Birmingham
Birmingham, Alabama

Sharon Borbon
Executive Assistant to the Provost
California Institute of Technology
Pasadena, California

Henry Brenzenoff
Acting Dean
University of Medicine and
    Dentistry of New Jersey
Graduate School of Biomedical
    Sciences
Newark, New Jersey

Jerry Bryant
Director, Science Education
 Initiatives
United Negro College Fund
Fairfax, Virginia

Henry Bryant
National Institutes of Health
Bethesda, Maryland

Joan Burrelli
Senior Analyst
National Science Foundation
Arlington, Virginia

Roger Chalkley
Senior Associate Dean for
 Biomedical Research
Vanderbilt University Medical Center
Nashville, Tennessee

Joan Chesney
Professor of Pediatrics
University of Tennessee, Memphis
Memphis, Tennessee

Daryl E. Chubin
Senior Policy Officer
National Science Board
National Science Foundation
Arlington, Virginia

Mary Clark
Associate Dean for Faculty Affairs
Harvard Medical School
Boston, Massachusetts

Deborah Cohen
Coordinator of Student and
 Postdoctoral Training Programs
National Institutes of Health
Office of Education
Bethesda, Maryland

Michael Cowan
Associate Dean for Student Services
Stanford Medical School
Stanford, California

Charles Craig
Interim Associate Dean for Research
West Virginia University
School of Medicine
Morgantown, West Virginia

Kyle Cunningham
Postdoctoral Affairs Coordinator
University of California, Los Angeles
Los Angeles, California

Rebecca Custer
Program Administrator
Jet Propulsion Laboratory
Pasadena, California

Aphi Daigler
Programs Coordinator
Division of Biological Sciences
University of Chicago

Susan Duby
Director, Division of Graduate
 Education
National Science Foundation
Arlington, Virginia

Alicia Dustira
Deputy Director, Division of Policy
 and Education
Department of Health and Human
 Services
Rockville, Maryland

Seznec Erwan
Scientific Assistant
Embassy of France
Washington, DC

Di Fang
Manager of Demographic and
    Workforce Studies
Association of American Medical
    Colleges
Washington, DC

Robert Fellows
Professor and Head
University of Iowa College of
    Medicine
Iowa City, Iowa

Gil Gilbert
Association Dean, Graduate School
Baylor College of Medicine
Houston, Texas

Mary Golladay
Program Director
Human Resources Statistics Program
National Science Foundation
Arlington, Virginia

Sharon Gordon
Director, Office of Education
National Institute of Dental and
    Craniofacial Research
National Institutes of Health
Bethesda, Maryland

Michael Gottesman
Deputy Director for Intramural
    Research
National Institutes of Health
Bethesda, Maryland

Gerald Grunwald
Professor and Associate Dean
College of Graduate Studies
Thomas Jefferson University
Philadelphia, Pennsylvania

Jong-on Hahm
Director, Committee on Women in
    Science and Engineering
The National Academies
Washington, DC

Bridgitte Harrison
Coordinator
University of Cincinnati
Cincinnati, Ohio

Robert Hershey
Consulting Engineer
Robert L. Hershey, PE
Washington, DC

Janet Hom
Administrator, Office of Postdoctoral
    and Graduate Training
Postdoc and Graduate Affairs
Baylor College of Medicine
Houston, Texas

Jack Hsia
Chief, Academic Affairs
National Institute of Standards and
    Technology
Gaithersburg, Maryland

Martin Ionescu-Pioggia
Officer
Burroughs Wellcome Fund
Research Triangle Park, North
    Carolina

Eric Iverson
Public Policy Associate
American Society for Engineering
    Education
Washington, DC

Nirmala Kannankutty
National Science Foundation
Division of Science Resources Studies
Human Resources Statistics Program
Arlington, Virginia

Kevin Kelley
California State University, Long
  Beach
Department of Biological Sciences
Long Beach, California

Mohammad Khoshnevisan
National Institute of Dental and
  Craniofacial Research
National Institutes of Health
Bethesda, Maryland

Lisa Kozlowski
Post Doc Fellow
Johns Hopkins University
Baltimore, Maryland

Jean Labus
Sr. Personnel Representative
Postdoctoral Program Coordinator
Eli Lilly Company
Indianapolis, Indiana

Susan Lord
National Institutes of Health
Deputy Director, Training and
  Education
National Cancer Institute Clinical
  Division
Bethesda, Maryland

Robert Mahley
President
The J. David Gladstone Institutes
San Francisco, California

Mary McCormick
Senior Program Analyst
Howard Hughes Medical Institute
Chevy Chase, Maryland

Richard McGee
Associate Dean for Student Affairs
Mayo Graduate School
Rochester, Minnesota

Linda Meadows
Assistant VP for Research
Ohio State University
Columbus, Ohio

Vid Mohan-Ram
Science Writer
Science's Next Wave
1200 New York Avenue, NW
Washington, DC

You-Hyun Moon
Science Counselor
Korean Embassy
Washington, DC

Mayumi Naramura
Visiting Fellow
National Institute of Allergy and
  Infectious Diseases
National Institutes of Health
Rockville, Maryland

Norine Noonan
Assistant Administrator
Research and Development
US Environmental Protection
  Agency
Washington, DC

Joel Oppenheim
Associate Dean, Director
Sackler Institute, New York
    University
School of Medicine
New York, New York

Roslyn Orkin
Assistant Dean for Faculty Affairs
Harvard Medical School
Boston, Massachusetts

Sonia Ortega
Program Director
National Science Foundation
Division of Graduate Education
Arlington, Virginia

Arti Patel
Pre-Doctoral Intramural Research
    Training Award Program
National Institute of Environmental
    Sciences
Research Triangle Park, North
    Carolina

Trevor Penning
Associate Dean
Postdoctoral Research Training
University of Pennsylvania School
    of Medicine
Philadelphia, Pennsylvania

Philip Perlman
Associate Dean, Southwest Grad
    School
University of Texas Southwest
    Medical Center
Dallas, Texas

Michael Princiotta
Post Doc Fellow
National Institute of Allergy and
    Infectious Diseases
National Institutes of Health
Bethesda, Maryland

Stephen Quigley
Science Policy and Management
    Consultant
Washington, DC

Rao Mrinalini
Associate Dean, Graduate College
University of Illinois at Chicago
Chicago, Illinois

Alan Rapoport
Senior Analyst
Division of Science Resources
    Studies
National Science Foundation
Arlington, Virginia

Ian Reynolds
Department of Pharmacology
The University of Pittsburgh
Pittsburgh, Pennsylvania

Susan Rich
Director, Office of Postdoc Education
Emory University School of Medicine
Atlanta, Georgia

Robert Rich
Manager, Professional Services
American Chemical Society
Washington, DC

Monique Rijnkels
President, Postdoctoral Association
Baylor College of Medicine
Houston, Texas

John Russell
Associate Dean of Graduate
    Education
Washington University Medical
    School
St. Louis, Missouri

Walter Schaffer
National Institutes of Health
Research Training Officer
Bethesda, Maryland

Dennis Shields
Professor, Developmental and
    Molecular Biology
Albert Einstein College of Medicine
Bronx, New York

Allan Shipp
Assistant Vice President
Biomedical and Health Science
    Research
Association of American Medical
    Colleges
Washington, DC

Charles Shuler
Director and Professor
University of Southern California
Center for Craniofacial Molecular
    Biology
Los Angeles, California

Chris Simmons
Federal Relations Officer
Association of American Universities
Washington, DC

Patricia Sokolove
Associate Dean, Graduate School
University of Maryland, Baltimore
Baltimore, Maryland

Peter Syverson
Vice President
Research and Information Services
Council of Graduate Sciences
Washington, DC

Michael Teitelbaum
Program Director
Alfred P. Sloan Foundation
New York, New York

Philippe Tondeur
Director
Division of Mathematical Sciences
National Science Foundation
Arlington, Virginia

Jim Voytuk
Project Officer
Office of Scientific Engineering and
    Personnel
The National Academies
Washington, DC

Robin Wagner
Associate Director of Graduate
    Services
Career and Placement Services
University of Chicago
Chicago, Illinois

Valerie Williams
RAND Corporation
Washington, DC

Pauline Wong
Post Doc Fellow
Johns Hopkins School of Medicine
Biological Chemical Department
Baltimore, Maryland

Letitia Yao
Research Associate
University of Minnesota
Minneapolis, Minnesota

Jonathan Yewdell
Chief, Cellular Biology Section
National Institute of Allergy and
    Infectious Diseases
National Institutes of Health
Bethesda, Maryland

Tamara Zemlo
Policy Analyst
Federation of American Societies
    for Experimental Biology
Bethesda, Maryland

Janet Zinser
Associate Director, School of
    Medicine
Office of Postdoc Programs
University of Pennsylvania
Philadelphia, Pennsylvania

Daniel Zuckerman
President, Johns Hopkins Postdoc
    Association
School of Medicine, Johns Hopkins
    University
Baltimore, Maryland

Appendix E

Summary of Results from Institutional Focus Groups

The rapid growth of the postdoctoral population is a recent phenomenon, occurring mostly since the late 1980s. As a result, relatively little has been published about the incorporation of postdoctoral scholars into the research enterprise. Therefore COSEPUP augmented its study with an unusual degree of on-site investigation and interviewing via 39 focus groups. The majority of post-docs were held with postdocs and/or advisers at eleven universities, seven national labs, two private institutes, and three industrial labs. When possible, staff met separately with postdocs and advisers in order to allow free expression of views; at some sites only postdocs were available. In addition, several focus groups were held at federal and nonfederal funding organizations.

The following institutions assisted the staff in this process:

Universities: Caltech, University of Chicago, Howard University, Johns Hopkins School of Medicine, Massachusetts Institute of Technology, University of Pennsylvania, University of Pittsburgh, North Carolina State University, Stanford University, University of Maryland at Baltimore.

National labs and agencies: Argonne National Laboratory, Goddard Space Flight Center (NASA), Jet Propulsion Laboratory, National Institutes of Health, National Institute of Standards and Technology (NIST), Naval Research Laboratory, National Science Foundation.

Private institutes: RAND Corporation.

Industrial labs: Genentech, Eli Lilly, Microsoft.

Funding Organizations: Howard Hughes Medical Institute, National Science Foundation, National Institutes of Health

The meeting at North Carolina State was also attended by postdocs from the US Department of Energy's Triangle Universities Nuclear Laboratory, Glaxo-Wellcome pharmaceuticals, Duke University, and the University of North Carolina.

The focus groups with postdocs and advisers established many of the primary themes of this guide. Each meeting followed a standardized format, in which participants were asked to review the then-current draft of the guide, contribute their experiences and opinions on major points of the guide, and suggest recommendations and "best practices." Some points were raised by participants at virtually every meeting (especially concerns about compensation, institutional status, and mentoring); other points were particular to specific fields, sectors, and individuals.

This summary presents a list of dominant themes, as well as a brief sampling of experiences and opinions from participants. During the course of the study, more extensive summaries of individual focus groups were drawn up after the meetings and constituted an extensive body of information on which COSEPUP based its deliberations.

DOMINANT THEMES

Professional Status

- With regard to their standing as researchers, postdocs seldom consider themselves "students." They feel they are skilled practitioners who may know as much or more about their work as their advisers and therefore should be considered junior colleagues.
- At the same time, postdocs say they have much to learn about their profession before they can be considered independent researchers. Depending on their career objectives, postdocs may have to learn such professional skills as grant proposal writing, lab management, writing papers, reviewing the work of peers, mentoring others in the lab, and teaching full courses.
- At some organizations, postdocs say they are still regarded as "glorified students" and have yet to gain the respect they deserve.
- Attaining full professional status may occur slowly, if the postdoc seldom leaves the research facility, or more quickly, if the adviser provides opportunities to interact with others, to take on new responsibilities, and to understand the context and traditions of research.

- Many postdocs are confused about expectations. Said one: "I came here expecting to learn, but I find I am judged only by my output."
- Postdocs are learning to be independent, but many see the need for more guidance than they receive to avoid "chasing down dead ends."

The social sciences have been slower to accept the need for postdoctoral training than the physical and life sciences, and some prejudice exists against postdoctoral positions. Postdocs in the field feel a postdoc can launch their career more quickly and learn to write proposals.

Administrative Structures for Postdocs

- Most postdocs are hired directly by researchers without going through institutional personnel procedures; thus they may be "institutionally invisible." The may either lack institutional benefits or be uninformed about their rights.
- Few institutions have centralized offices or officers designated to address issues of concern to postdocs, clarify policies, or answer questions.
- Many foreign postdocs receive little or no orientation before or after arrival, and waste considerable time and energy searching for answers to relatively straightforward questions about visa requirements and American culture.
- Most postdocs do not receive a contractual letter of appointment that addresses such important issues as length of appointment, benefits offered, salary, intellectual property policy, and terms of completion.
- Postdocs at national and industrial facilities were generally better paid than academic postdocs, fit more easily into an employment/benefits category (such as temporary or contractual employee), receive better infrastructure support and more travel funding, and had fewer complaints about their supervision or recognition. Many, however, worried about their job prospects.

Compensation and Benefits

- Postdocs in certain fields, notably the life sciences, feel that their pay level is insufficient given their advanced level of skill and experience. They often pointed to higher pay scales for postdocs with MD degrees and for technical staff with less experience and/or lower degrees.
- Wide variations in pay (examples of stipend levels reported to the committee range from $14,000 in the case of a postdoc on a foreign grant to $60,000+ for some postdocs at national labs) are usually unrelated to the skill or experience of the recipient.
- Postdocs performing similar work at the same institutions may also

receive different benefits, depending on their source of support. The 40 percent or so of postdocs who are supported by federal fellowships, federal traineeships, and nonfederal (including foreign) sources may or may not receive benefits, while the 60 percent or so of postdocs who are supported on research grants usually receive standard institutional benefits.

- Funding organizations and institutions often disagree about who bears primary responsibility for setting funding levels. Funding organizations point out that institutions or principal investigators may determine how much to pay their postdocs, but institutions often follow the lead of the largest funding organizations (notably the NIH) in making those determinations.

Classification and Titles

- At some academic institutions postdocs are "unclassified" and have no institutional status. Institutions classify and treat them in various ways: as "students" (notably at Stanford, to allow universal provision of benefits), "staff" (common at national and industrial labs), "employees" (those who are paid under research grants may or may not have titles, although they usually receive the same institutional benefits as employees), and occasionally "faculty" (common in mathematics, for example).
- Some institutions place limits on the time a researcher can be a postdoc; most universities do not. Some postdocs continue working for many years (ten years is not unusual in physics) without acquiring regular institutional status or qualifying for matching retirement benefits.
- Many postdocs complain about their invisibility, that "no one outside the lab knows who we are."

Career Planning and Transitions

- Many postdocs would like more information about careers, especially nonacademic careers, but have little time to find good sources.
- Most institutions have no central career planning service for postdocs, who must rely on the knowledge of their adviser or other research colleagues for guidance.
- Few advisers assist postdocs in acquiring outside-the-lab career skills such as teaching, writing, public speaking, coursework, lab management, or grant preparation.
- Many postdocs don't know their adviser's policy on attending valuable professional meetings and are reluctant to ask.
- Many researchers look back on their postdoctoral appointment as a "once-in-a-lifetime chance" time to pick up skills and focus intently on research.
- Few postdocs in industry are hired by their institutions.

Postdoctoral Associations

- Some universities have supported (financially and logistically) postdocs' desire to form associations for the purpose of information sharing, social activities, and communication with the administration.
- These associations for the most part have developed good relationships with administrations, provided postdocs with a sense of community, and achieved many of their goals.
- Administration support is essential for the continuity of postdoctoral associations because the postdoctoral population is a transient one.
- Some postdocs described a need for a national postdoctoral association.

Foreign National and Minority Postdocs

- Postdocs who are non-US citizens often have poor postdoctoral experiences characterized by difficulties with language, funding, visa status, mentoring, and/or acculturation.
- At the same time, opportunities for networking and jobs are often greater in the US, and many postdocs would like to stay on in this country.
- Many foreign postdocs don't know where to find needed resources at their institution and receive little orientation when they arrive.
- Foreign postdocs have an easier and more productive time when institutions make their existing international offices available and known.
- Few postdocs are members of minority groups who are generally underrepresented in science and engineering (African-American, Native American, Hispanic). Very few representatives of these minority groups participated in the focus groups, so that COSEPUP was unable to gather sufficient information to comment on the probable causes of underrepresentation.

Mentoring and Evaluation

- There is little agreement among either postdocs or advisers about the adviser's obligation to serve as mentor. Most postdocs at universities express a need for mentoring and depend for this on a single faculty member. At national and industry facilities, mentors may or may not be significant because research settings tend to be more group oriented. Some members of both groups feel that postdocs should have the maturity to work things out on their own.
- Many postdocs choose a program in order to work with a particular mentor. At universities, in particular, they tend to identify their affiliation with that single person and may have no relationship to the host institution.

- Some postdocs seldom see their adviser and receive little guidance either in their technical work or in regard to their careers.
- Postdocs disagreed about the value of a "famous" adviser. Some were willing to endure a lack of mentoring for the advantage of being affiliated with a renowned researcher; others preferred an adviser with interpersonal skills.
- Some postdocs at the most prestigious universities had the most complaints about a lack of good mentoring.
- One postdoc described her adviser as outstanding because she helped her avoid "dead ends" in her research. Another praised his adviser for being flexible and offering freedom to explore.
- Principal investigators are rewarded primarily for their research (in grant renewals, promotions, and tenure), and less often get any credit for teaching or mentoring. With the many demands on their time, it is difficult to give high priority to mentoring postdocs, especially if it is not explicitly valued or required.
- A few institutions use "mentoring committees" comprised of several potential role models to expand the guidance, feedback, and perspective available to postdocs.
- Postdocs agreed that ethical concerns are very important. One told of being asked not to publish something that went against his adviser's work, and others agreed that this is not uncommon.
- A postdoc in industry may work on many different projects (unlike a postdoc in academia) under different advisers. Postdocs in industry still depend on their advisers for mentoring, career guidance, and expanding their professional network of contacts.

OTHER OPINIONS

From postdocs

- There was much discussion of how many job classifications exist, and how important they can be. "Fellows," in particular, complained about their lack of benefits, vis-a-vis "research associates."
- There were also many stories about the inequities of salaries and stipends, such as instances where lab directories gave very different amounts to equally qualified people for no apparent reason.
- Foreign postdocs on visas were adamant about the need for access to an office of international affairs to help with visa problems, of which many were described. Many voiced objections to using the J1 (student) visa for postdocs, saying the H1B is more appropriate. The H1 status is very difficult to get, however.

- Many postdocs in academia felt faculty were "not responsive" to the concerns of postdocs—even those who had been postdocs themselves.
- Several institutions were in the process of starting a postdoctoral association. They were using other models (UCSF, Johns Hopkins, Einstein) and praised their value.
- A postdoc in mathematics is unusual. Such a postdoc is usually hired in a university faculty slot and teaches a full load, receives little mentoring, and is paid better than average.
- Many suggested that problems are inherent in the imbalance of power in favor of the adviser.
- The importance of good relations with the adviser: "They're your advocate in the field. Without them you don't have a chance."
- What is lacking in postdoctoral training is not bench skills, but other professional skills.
- One reason it's difficult to get a job is that job offers are very specific, requiring a particular technical skill.
- Most said they were postdocs because they loved science, but that they deserved a living wage.
- Many agreed that "social isolation" was a serious problem for postdocs.
- Many agreed that there are too many graduate students, not enough jobs, and "something should be done to keep the numbers down."
- There are subtle pressures to stay in the lab as late as everyone else. Some women felt they could not have children while doing a postdoc.
- Some postdocs said that funding agencies may unintentionally discourage having children by setting time limits after the PhD for applying for funds.
- Most felt that travel to meetings is essential for establishing a necessary reputation, network, and ultimately independence.
- A number of postdocs recommended the elimination of the "postdoc" category in favor of "scholars" or some other name. Many felt that even a productive postdoctoral appointment was a "holding pattern" compared to a "real" job.
- Some recommended the elimination of postdocs as a category, to be replaced by various forms of employment.
- Many felt they were being used as technicians and not really encouraged to learn new skills and areas.
- Postdocs at a leading industry lab felt they were more than trainees: "We're proving ourselves, and learning new skills."
- Some postdocs at industrial labs felt they had a greater variety of stimulating research opportunities than postdocs at universities and more freedom to choose their research areas, although their work still had to support the theme of their mentor's work.
- Other reported advantages of an industry postdoc: learning how industry

works (more teamwork), "fewer hassles," great resources (generous budget, technical help, travel funds), a more "sane" working environment than academia.

- Postdocs at national labs often like to maintain an academic connection, which makes it easier to return to academia.
- Work at national labs tends to be more practical than at universities.
- Many postdocs in national labs desired more help with 1) grant writing, 2) managerial skills, and 3) mentoring.
- Some national labs are group oriented, with groups making decisions about research and whom to hire. The group leader's job was described as "running interference for you and letting you do your work."
- Some postdocs at national and industrial labs missed the fun of working with students and passing along their knowledge.

From advisers

- Postdocs need more recognition that they and their work are important.
- The vast majority of postdoctoral experiences are good, but for those that aren't, each institution must recognize the problem and strive to do better.
- Faculty do want postdocs to have an educational experience, but this doesn't always occur in practice.
- Some advisers warned that if universities don't treat postdocs more "humanely," they will not be able to attract the "best and brightest" to academia.
- Other advisers favor a more "free market" approach, whereby researchers follow the most interesting opportunities, including those in the private sector.
- The primary responsibility of the postdoc is research performance.
- An increase in salary for postdocs would only fuel the fundraising efforts of faculty.
- Faculty felt that evaluation does happen, and that the criteria for advancement are clear to postdocs as well as faculty. "They know," said one. "The clock is running as soon as they arrive." Said another: "You can quantify their progress by what they do."
- Said one adviser: "When people are doing well, they don't complain; when they don't do well, they look for a reason. We also see that with faculty who don't get tenure."
- One adviser said the most serious conflicts occur over credit, who gets to give a paper, and harassment (i.e., general rather than sexual). In multi-group collaborations, conflicts are common over sharing credit.

From institutions

- Institutions have the responsibility to establish a central office or officer to coordinate postdoctoral affairs.
- The primary advantage of a centralized office is to provide structure and standardization of policies and procedures, as well as a clearinghouse for information for postdocs.
- Institutions have a responsibility to provide some level of job placement/ career services.
- The institution's role in supporting a postdoctoral association for post-docs is crucial because postdocs are a transient population.
- Most institutions follow the lead of the NIH in setting stipend/salary levels.
- Prior to recent years, few universities had mechanisms for tracking, supporting, or even counting the members of their postdoctoral populations.
- Some institutions raise the levels of classification and compensation of postdocs according to the number of years in that position; beyond a certain time (e.g., 4-5 years) a "postdoc" moves to a new "track" with retirement and other employee benefits.
- One university system created a new category for postdocs so they could receive benefits (through the Graduate School).

From funding organizations

- Advisers sometimes classify postdocs in different ways to fit the varying requirements of funding organizations.
- In the view of some funding organizations, the variability in classification is not a bad thing: "The system needs flexibility to operate."
- Some officials at federal funding organizations are reluctant to specify the status of postdocs at various institutions, or otherwise dictate how grant money should be used. "We don't want to be seen as intrusive."
- The NSF has begun a more explicit effort to encourage good mentoring in recent years, primarily through the general tone and specific requirements of its research grant application forms.
- The NIH encourages good mentoring by requiring information about the careers of postdocs who have worked in a particular adviser's lab.
- Under NIH guidelines, postdocs who are fellows or trainees are paid directly by NIH; postdocs who are supported under research grants are not paid directly; instead, the grant money goes to the institution, which determines compensation and benefits.
- The NIH does not require training on ethics, and gives universities a lot of latitude on the form, content, and amount of training.
- Some federal program officers are reluctant to set specific criteria for

mentoring (e.g., to require periodic evaluations of postdocs) because of anticipated resistance: "It would be a burden on the investigator, who would just generate a standard paragraph of text." These officers suggest an alternative strategy: to make clear that postdocs require training, and to allow advisers to determine the most appropriate methods.

GENERAL POINT

- Not surprisingly, the perceptions of postdocs often differed from those of faculty. Many postdocs, especially at universities, expressed dissatisfaction with established practices of mentoring, compensation, recognition, and career development, and were pessimistic about their job prospects. Faculty, while often sympathetic, tended to say that a good postdoctoral experience is the responsibility of the postdoc, and that those who are qualified and do their work will find the right jobs.